High-Tech Worship?

High-Tech Worship?

Using Presentational Technologies Wisely

Quentin J. Schultze

A Division of Baker Book House Co
Grand Rapids, Michigan 49516

Published by Baker Books
a division of Baker Publishing Group
P.O. Box 6287, Grand Rapids, MI 49516-6287
www.bakerbooks.com

Second printing, January 2005

Printed in the United States of America

Library of Congress Cataloging-in-Publication Data
Schultze, Quentin J. (Quentin James), 1952–
High-tech worship? : using presentational technologies wisely / Quentin J. Schultze.
p. cm.
Includes bibliographical references.
ISBN 0-8010-6480-5 (pbk.)
1. Public worship—Audio-visual aids. I. Title.
BV288.S38 2004
264′.0028′4—dc22 2003018386

To Barbara
who shows me how to dance faithfully in the liturgy of life

And to Pastor Jack Roeda
who helps me dance in step with the gospel

Contents

Helpful Lists

Acknowledgments

I am indebted to many people for their insights, advice, and wisdom.

John D. Witvliet, director of the Calvin Institute of Christian Worship, enthusiastically encouraged me to venture into this field. Many other Institute staff helped as well, including Kristen Verhulst, Cindy Holtrop, Kathy Smith, Betty Grit, Joyce Borger, Lisa Vander Molen, and Emily Cooper. The Lilly Endowment provided funding through the Worship Institute.

David Wood, former associate director of the Louisville Institute, has been particularly helpful.

Steve Koster's survey research, also funded by the Worship Institute, helped us to understand American churches' use of technology. I have included some of the results in this book (see appendix).

During the summer of 2003 the Institute and the Calvin Seminars in Christian Scholarship program sponsored a weeklong workshop on technology and ministry. Participants reviewed the manuscript with charity and good sense: co-leader Duane Kelderman, Robb Redman, Rev. Lee Zachman, Thomas DeVries, Bernie Bakker, Jack B. Dik, David L. Heilman, A. R. Neal Mathers, Brian Fuller, Tony Koeman, Brent Wassink, Doug Thompson, Rick Wolling, Christopher Eads, Miyoung Paik, Bea M. Callery, David Bowden, and Alida van Dijk.

Bob Hosack, Chad Allen, Cheryl Van Andel, and Brian Brunsting of Baker Book House served me ably as editors and designers.

Calvin College's president, Gaylen Byker, and my department chair, Randall Bytwerk, blessed me with their support and friendship. Our able assistant in the Department of Communication Arts and Sciences, Yvonne Posthuma, serves with joy and delight.

Additional colleagues and friends who gave me important advice include Helen Sterk, Ronda Oosterhoff, Todd Johnson, Emily Brink, Eileen D. Horak, Doug Lawrence, Paul Vander Klay, Bob Keeley, James Zwier, Dean Kladder, Rev. Paul E. Detterman, Mark Schemper, Cindy de Jong, Ron Rienstra, Laura Smit, Doug Brouwer, and Ed Seely.

My wife, Barbara, shows me how to live in grace. Bless her soul. And bless the Triune One who created her with a heart for the dance of life.

Introduction

> The ubiquitous overhead projector has found its way from the bowling alley to the classroom to the worship center.[1]
>
> —Robert Phillips

My wife and I were living in west Florida during a nine-month sabbatical. Every week we visited a different church to participate in worship across the denominational spectrum.

We were surprised to discover that most congregations were using *presentational technologies*, from simple text and images projected on a screen (e.g., PowerPoint presentations) to movie clips and congregationally produced videos.

Sadly, there seemed to be little thought behind the flurry of technological activity. Some visual presentations were aesthetically impoverished, reflecting poor layout and design. Others were not connected to the worship theme or biblical text. Song lyrics occasionally were hard to read or were not projected in time with the music. Worst of all, the presentations frequently did not flow seamlessly with worship; they detracted from the overall *liturgy* (the "doing" of worship), drawing attention to the screen instead of God.

Moreover, the placement of projection screens at times covered worthy liturgical art and clashed with architectural style and interior decoration. Sometimes the screen had become the focus of worship. Worship was watching a screen for an hour.

"How could this happen?" I wondered repeatedly during that year.

Fortunately, we also experienced some wonderful, inspiring, and appropriate worship presentations, even in small churches with very limited budgets. By the end of the sabbatical we had witnessed a very mixed bag of excellent and mediocre high-tech worship.

Presentational technologies can shape worship for both good and bad. The key in using presentational technologies wisely is employing them well in a service of worthy purposes, not for their own ends. We should not use technology for the sake of technology but in support of commendable worship.

A large industry promotes the use of electronic and now digital projection technologies in worship. This industry sometimes promises more than it is able to deliver. New communication technologies can both facilitate and interfere with communication, depending on when, why, how, and how well they are used. Just buying and installing equipment will not automatically enhance worship.

Given human nature, new technologies are always mixed blessings. In one of the great ironies of our age, new communication technologies are making it increasingly difficult for us to *commune* with one another—to get to know and love one another. Who has the time? We're too busy scrambling from one technology or message to the next one. Some congregations simply replicate this frenetic pace in worship services.

Recently I spoke to a congregation that had installed a large projection screen at the front of the church, directly over a large wooden cross that for decades had greeted everyone who entered the sanctuary. I was surprised to discover that it was not a motorized screen, although it could be retracted manually by a person standing on a ladder. The two young men who were posting hymn numbers for the upcoming evening service told me that the congregation seldom retracts it. "What about the cross behind the screen?" I asked them. "Well," they responded, "we solved that problem by projecting a little cross on the bottom of the screen during worship."

Then I noticed a microphone for choral pickup hung from the ceiling in front of the screen. "Does it cast a shadow on the screen when the projector is on?" I queried. "Yeah," one of them responded, "but we're used to it."

Here was a church that was trying to enter the twenty-first century with the latest technology. I am grateful for the church's courage. On the other hand, I was dismayed that the congregation had not solved some fundamental problems before moving ahead.

We get into these kinds of problems usually because (1) we innovate too quickly, (2) we lose track of the overarching purpose (in this case, worshiping God), or (3) we fail to include in our planning the range of people and talents that we need to use technology wisely.

When I gather with members of my congregation in a circle around the communion table, I am reminded that worship is for everyone, the young and old, the newly converted and the saints of old, the short and the tall, the technologically skilled and the technologically challenged.

In this book I give these and other voices a hearing, because wisdom about using technology well in worship requires multiple perspectives.

My thesis is that *liturgical* wisdom (i.e., wisdom about how to plan, order, and conduct worship) should direct how we employ presentational technologies. As stewards of worship who seek to express our love of God in praise and thanksgiving, we should *adapt* technology to authentic, meaningful, and God-glorifying worship. The love of the Lord is foundational to all true worship (John 4:23). Technology should nurture such love.

1

Our Confusion

> In the world the theater is worship—in Christendom the churches are. Is there a difference?[1]
>
> —Søren Kierkegaard

Ivan Illich, a wise critic of technological excess, refused for years to speak in any venue that required audio amplification. He simply declined to use a microphone because it tends to lead to larger, less humane scales of communication. He called for "convivial" forms of human dialogue over impersonal communication.[2]

Illich's argument is too anti-technological, but there is wisdom in his point that we need to discern how to use new technologies appropriately. In contemporary society technological innovation takes on a life of its own, as if faster, more impressive, and more efficient technologies are always better.

Our High-Tech Lives

Living in a technological society, we have to learn again and again how to use new devices well. I use a computer every day, but I am not always sure how it works or what to do when it does not. I struggle to understand both the technical and the nontechnical aspects of communication technologies. Some days I seem to lose the battle in frustration. I miscommunicate with or offend others, mistakenly causing grief.

We also find ourselves bombarded with messages through all kinds of new technologies, from the Internet to cell phones, voicemail to satellite television. The pace of messaging continues to increase in our lives, causing us to jump from one message to another and to spend less time with each person. Some people rejoice, saying we are learning to "multitask," but this seems a bit optimistic. "Our bodies move," writes one observer, "but their movements are frenetic. Everywhere we look in society we find many people pulled in too many directions at once, never really able to live peacefully in the present moment."[3]

Increasingly we face lives of multimedia, multi-messaging, and multi-confusion. This might convince us to slow down enough to reconsider how high-tech we want our lives to be. Is the church contributing to thoughtless innovation? Is worship, in particular, better off if it pursues high-tech "progress"? Should worship by nature be less high-tech and more high-touch? Or is there a place for high-tech worship that is humbly done, thoughtful, beautiful, and presumably pleasing to God? I think so.

Worship and Technology

Often there is a fine line between revolutionizing and uprooting *liturgical practices* (the ways we order and conduct worship). Sometimes worship leaders tell me that using presentational technologies in their churches is a no-brainer because they "do not use liturgies." What they really mean is that they do not rely upon *formal* liturgical practices such as responsive readings, collective prayers, and creedal recitations.

All corporate worship is based at least implicitly on a liturgy. A church might replace the greeting "The Lord be with you"

Presentational Technologies

Presentational technologies enable people to project still and moving images, from song lyrics to video clips, on a screen in small to very large settings such as auditoriums and stadiums.

with something as simple as "good morning," but the congregation is still participating in liturgy. Liturgy is composed of the "works" the body of believers do together in order to worship. The *ways* a body of believers conducts such an effort—e.g., a greeting, confession, celebration, affirmation, proclamation, offering, and benediction—is its liturgy.

Churches modify liturgies over time so that worship remains relevant and meaningful to congregants. But to "revolutionize" liturgical practices (i.e., wholesale change, top to bottom, with no continuity with the past) is to risk dismantling worship and even forgetting how to worship. Moreover, if there are some time-proven, biblically affirmed liturgical practices—as I believe there are—then we ought not to disregard them even as we rightly reformulate liturgy for new cultural settings. A congregation might discover even better liturgical practices by putting aside older ways of worshiping. Nevertheless, all corporate worship requires some communal memory and shared ritual (recurring practices)—two things technological societies tend to dismiss as old-fashioned or oppressive.

I am not suggesting that we remove from worship all presentational technologies. Worship always relies upon human skills and techniques, if not upon particular technologies. Worshipers have long fashioned raw materials into such worship artifacts as chalices, stained glass, candles, incense, and crosses. Worship is necessarily liturgical *and* technological.

The questions we face in today's high-tech milieu are actually age-old: What kinds of liturgical (and technological) practices are most fitting for worship—*when, where, how, for whom, by whom,* and *why*? And to answer such questions we must grasp the significance of both technology *and* worship. We need to reach beyond our pragmatic biases (do what "works" right now!) to engage both tradition (the principles underlying past worship, as evident in the Scriptures and in the history of the church) and other cultures where the gospel is communicated vibrantly and the church is growing through the work of the Spirit.[4]

The church is growing the fastest in areas such as Latin America and Africa where advanced technology is comparatively limited. Our technological assumptions are deeply cultural. It is right to want worship to be relevant to the people of God; it is entirely different to assume that worship must reflect the technological biases of a particular culture, whether it is high-tech or high-touch.

Why Churches Decide to Use "Media" in Worship

84% more relevance to our members
77% more relevance to youth
66% seeker sensitivity/evangelism
59% technically gifted people (available in congregation)
61% avoiding books
59% exploring art in worship
38% cheap gear available
33% keeping pace with other churches[5]

Not long ago I worshiped in a small monastery in Massachusetts that is very low-tech. The chapel is like a small cathedral with only a few rows of seating on three sides. There was no audio amplification to broadcast the harmonious antiphonal singing of the seventeen brothers. I found the intimacy a bit unnerving because everyone could see everyone else's face, but I also found it deeply engaging because I was able to participate meaningfully in the songs and readings even though I had never attended previously.

The simple (not simplistic) liturgy was both easy to follow and profoundly gospel oriented in that it conveyed the mystery of grace. The three-sided seating space connoted equal relations among worshipers. The fourth side suggested a reverent relationship with God.

I would never recommend that everyone should worship in this monastic way. On the other hand, contemporary churches ought not ignore the age-old liturgical practices that occur in such intimate settings. We can learn from this community of monks about worship just as they might learn something from us about using advanced technologies in worship. In fact, I discovered that the brothers had rewritten their "rules for living" in recent years to reformulate their traditions for a new era in human history.

This monastic community's "rule" for the "daily office" (the periods of worship) reads, "The Daily Office is a sustained act of union with Christ by which we participate in his unceasing offering of love to the Father. In reciting the psalms, singing canticles and hymns, proclaiming the divine word in Scripture, or lifting our voices in prayer, we are to enter more and more into the mind, heart, and will of Christ, and to be borne up by the Spirit in him to the Father. . . . As we sing and chant deep levels of our being are involved; our hearts are lifted up in greater exultation. And music enhances our worship with riches inherited from many ages."[6] That's a remarkably good description of fitting worship and one that most of us could adopt for worship settings in which we use presentational technologies.

Our Image-Ignorant Culture

Many cultural changes precipitate the rush in some churches to high-tech worship. Perhaps foremost is the assumption that the most effective worship today must be visually augmented with presentational technologies. Some observers of contemporary North America suggest that for young people electronic images are the new "language."[7] The future of worship, they conclude, depends on how effectively churches can employ digital and electronic technologies to capture the visual imaginations of youth. These advocates say that the church must learn to compete visually with the popular arts, such as film and television.

One supporter says that "visual imagery is the primary language of our day and draws together people of all ages, races, genders, and classes." He adds that the "language of the visual arts" enables people to "communicate effectively to younger, visually oriented generations."[8] Another one contends that the projection screen "is the stained glass, and the cross, for the electronic media age . . . constantly transposing new imagery before us. Icons were the Bible for the illiterate, and the screen is the Bible for the post-literate."[9]

A pastor experienced in using presentational technologies in worship sees the need for visual worship as a natural response to the shift from print-oriented to image-oriented communication. He writes, "Our native worship language is expressed in printed

High-Tech Worship

High-tech worship relies extensively on computer-based presentational technologies, from still and animated slides created in programs like PowerPoint to video recordings and live video projection piped to screens in the sanctuary and in other locations, such as the nursery and narthex.

words and oral communication, while the new language of the 21st century, which has not quite made it into our worship, is expressed with visual imagery and popular music punctuated with short bursts of spoken information."[10]

Clearly North American society has gone through somewhat of a shift from a "print culture" to an "electronic culture" in the period since World War II. Most North Americans spend more of their daily time consuming moving-image media than they do reading, apart from work. Any serious discussion about "our native worship language," however, requires a historical perspective.

Christian practices from the beginning were visual.[11] One source describes early baptism as follows: "The candidate stood naked in the water, vowed to reject Satan, confessed faith in the Trinity, and was immersed three times under water. After being clothed again, the candidate was anointed with holy oil and received prayer with the laying on of hands."[12] The sacrament of the Lord's Supper was witnessed visually, too. By the third century the sharing of the Eucharist was *the* essential visual symbol of unity in Christ.[13] Churches similarly used nonsacramental visualizations, including stained-glass images of the gospel narrative, public morality plays, and other visual techniques to communicate the faith.

Christians have the freedom to integrate visual and aural symbols creatively into corporate worship. From this perspective, the recent interest in using presentational technologies to create worship art is a welcome renewal of something that the church has embraced for two millennia. Nevertheless, we face a major problem: we do not live in an *image-savvy* culture. We must contend with an *image-saturated* yet largely *image-ignorant* society. Our lives are *image-intense,* and undoubtedly movies and commercials have an enormous impact on young and old alike. But at the same time we are not very astute about how images communicate.

The church's task with respect to the use of presentational technologies in worship is enormous. We have to reeducate Christians about the importance of the visual in life as well as in the life of faith. In this task we can learn from the church's past as well as from contemporary media industries. Worship at the monastery was extraordinarily multimedia, as was worship in the early church, where the community depended on the intimacy and immediacy of the speaker-listener relationship, with the help of pitch, gestures, bodily posture, and audience responses.[14]

Unfortunately, some churches are not yet attuned to the importance of educating and worshiping with appropriate images. Some of today's sanctuaries and worship services are visually impoverished. They are stark places and events with few appealing adornments and little visual expression of the grandeur of God. Surely we do not require cathedrals to worship God well, but we do need something more than unadorned warehouses or lecture halls devoid of any signs of beauty and lacking any visual expressions of praise. Perhaps our image-ignorant culture runs wide and deep.

Young people need to know the meaning of worship and of particular liturgical practices more than they need to be entertained or visually mesmerized in worship. We all do. Presentational technologies will not magically transform us into a community of worshipers who love God and neighbor. Unless we use them wisely, attuned to how images contribute meaningfully to worship, they will tend to create even more visual "noise" that clutters our minds.

Communication vs. Transmission

Our confusion about the value of new media stems partly from the way we simplistically equate *transmission* with *communication*. Modern-day, mass-mediated society is indeed saturated with messengers and messages. All of this messaging, however, does not necessarily produce shared understandings. The word *communication* comes from the same root as that for the words *community* and *communion.*[15] Human communication is the action of communing with one another, not merely the business of sending and "consuming" messages. Studies of television viewers, for instance, find that most of them do not pay much attention to programs; stations *transmit* programs, but they do not necessarily *communicate* with viewers.

We can relieve boredom with the help of technological messaging much more easily than we can actually communicate. Deeper communication (communion) takes quite a bit of effort toward mutual understanding. In worship it requires a meaningful liturgy in which believers can participate wholeheartedly.

New communication technologies do not always improve human communication, no matter how we label them. One pastor rightly uses the concept of "multimedia communication" to describe what is possible with presentational technologies in worship. But he defines multimedia as "interactive digital media" arising out of a "synthesis of traditional forms of art and communication with rapidly evolving fields of computing and networking."[16] Stating that these new technologies are interactive does not make them so. Antiphonal singing or reading surely is interactive. Where is the inherent dialogue in a visual presentation? This is an important issue, particularly because, as I will address later, worship is dialogue.[17] Neither the transmission nor the reception (or "consumption") of messages is inherently interactive or dialogical.

We reside in a post-consumer society filled with images and words of all kinds, from those on pornographic websites to those in lavishly designed magazine advertisements. Our visually saturated culture is filled with evil as well as trivial noise that continually diverts our attention from anything important and makes it more difficult for us to focus on meaningful practices that carry eternal weight. Communication technologies can contribute to this confusion just as much as they can help us to overcome it.

Essential vs. Instrumental Worship

Most of the books I have read on using new communication technologies in worship wrongly assume worship is an *instrumental* rather than an *essential* practice. They mistakenly suggest that worship is about wowing audiences or competing with secular media. *Worship has its own, God-ordained purpose: gratefully expressing gratitude to the Creator in the most fitting means possible and inviting God's grace to move us to sacrificial lives of service.*

We need to view technologies in the context of the overarching purpose of worship. Getting this priority straight is a major challenge in the information age. Clearly we ought to desire worship that moves people to deeper intimacy with God, but at the same time we have to avoid trying to achieve this proudly as a testament to our own skill. We must begin with God's intrinsic designs for worship rather than with a mere human desire for technological efficiency and control—as if we could socially engineer perfect worship on our own without God.

Authentic worship is not about exercising human power as much as it is about receiving and expressing God's grace. When the human quest for control infects our worship, we tend to draw attention to ourselves and to create idols in our own image. The "reflexive nature of our existence," says one scholar, "ensures that we will become whatever it is that we worship. . . . If we worship technological 'making,' and if we view the world and others as 'devices' to be constructed and manipulated in the service of technical-rational ends, then we will view the quality and possibilities of our own existence in the same fashion."[18] A priest who emphasizes faithful living says that when you worship technology "you have God at your disposal. You have God in hand, we're in control. The temptation of religion always consists in turning the tables so that we ourselves take charge of the situation."[19]

Conclusion

Before we can use presentational technologies wisely in worship, we have to untangle our confusion over technology and worship. They are not the same thing. The former tends to create human hearts and minds bent on control, on manufacturing worship in tune with mere human desires. In contrast, worship calls us to remember who ultimately *is* in control. Worshipers depend on the Triune God for their very existence, their salvation, and their comfort in life.

This is partly why an understanding of liturgy is important for making decisions about using presentational technologies wisely today. The basic structure of Christian worship and living are the same: God speaks, human beings respond in faith. Our use of technology should support that kind of God-initiated worship.

2

Understanding Worship

> When we reflect on the built-in rhythm and repetition of the seasons of nature and biological life, we see a wonderful diversity in the Creator's design that helps us value both routine and diversity.[1]
>
> —Richard Winter

One worship magazine published an article titled "The Software Driven Church." The author contends that computerized churches "will begin to see a difference in the effectiveness of each area of church ministry."[2]

This kind of rhetoric often emanates from the church marketing industry, which hopes to sell liturgical products based on what such products supposedly can do for churches. But the most revealing aspect of these marketing publications is that they talk a lot about technology and little about the purpose of worship and ministry. They focus on the latest technologies, not on what makes for good worship. At times they seem to imply that the purpose of worship is manufacturing personal spiritual experiences.

Reading the church trade press reminds me that our technological era is marked by a preoccupation with human *means* and an evaporating sense of human *ends* (or purposes).[3] Surely we need to understand technological practices, but we have to consider such practices in the light of worship as a God-sanctioned activity, not a mere human creation. Today, however, we face a situation in which many believers know little about worship, its role in church life, and what makes for "good worship" in God's eyes. One national survey of churchgoers found that two-thirds were unable to describe to survey takers what worship is. Pollster George Barna called them "worship-challenged" Americans.[4]

Worship as Being Grateful and Giving Praise

I think the place to begin in understanding worship is to recognize it as a grateful response to what God has done and is doing in redemptive history. Worship is a natural response of praise to God as our Creator, Redeemer, and Comforter. We worship because we recognize by grace what God has done, is doing, and has promised to continue doing, namely, gathering the church as a redeemed community that carries the gospel message through time and space to every culture. He is our God; we are his people. God promises to carry through on his gift of salvation. Worship, therefore, is partly a memorial that enables us together to thank God for his "covenant fidelity."[5]

We engage in liturgical practices (i.e., we "do" worship) because they are a fitting response to the praiseworthy God of our salvation. What could be more natural than expressing our gratitude to God, in whom we have our being and through whom we celebrate together the joy of salvation? Ernest Gordon, a World War II American POW for years in Burma, recognized during his captivity that a person "need never be so defeated that he cannot do anything. Weak, sick, broken in body, far from home, and alone in a strange land, he can sing! He can worship!"[6] Gordon and his fellow prisoners realized what we often forget: God is with us through good and bad times, filling us with his mercies and leading us to give praise and thanks in worship.

Given this basis for worship as praise and thanksgiving, we can see why using some technologies carelessly is likely to become a problem. When we fail to see technology within the context of the power, majesty, and glory of God, we can become more enchanted with our technological ability than we are humbled by God's grace. We wrongly focus during worship on our liturgical accomplishments, on our technological skill and apparent power, rather than on what God has done, is doing, and has promised to complete through the salvation of covenant people. In worship we respond to "God the Creator."[7] God first created and now sustains all of creation. His creation enables us to engage in technological invention.

Technology itself does not obviate or overcome human sinfulness. Technologies are no better than the people using them. Arrogance about our technological abilities can weaken our desire to praise God gratefully and live humbly under God's perfect authority.

Worship Is Dialogue

Guided by the work of the Holy Spirit, we worship in dialogue with God and each other. "God fills the world with His speaking Voice," writes A. W. Tozer.[8] Participating in liturgy is a humble, obedient response to God.[9] Instead of breaking with wisdom and trying to discover our identity from within, we turn to God. The work of worship—liturgy—is responsive and reciprocal. Responding to God in gratitude sets up an ongoing relationship between the community of believers and the God of their salvation.

Seen this way, worship becomes a dialogic form of communion between God and God's people. God speaks. We listen and then respond. God speaks again. We respond to God and to each other. So goes the dialogue of worship. Worship becomes "the drama of a dialogue with God."[10]

This is especially important for us to consider when we address the role of presentational technologies in worship. How can we use them to equip believers to commune more fully with God and each other in our liturgical actions? We sometimes get into trouble when technologies situate us as an audience of individual spectators, not as a dialogical community. The value of some song lyrics projected on screens already has been proven

The Dialogue of Worship

The Creator-God spoke the world into existence. All creation responded with praise—and still does. The mountains declare God's glory. Human beings listen to God's Word of pardon, hear the mountains clapping, and respond fittingly with gratitude and praise. All worship is a dialogue among God and God's children, with the rest of creation in the choir. The Holy Spirit leads us to worship. Jesus Christ enables us to approach the Father. God says, "You are mine." God's people say, "Praise the Lord, O my soul!" May the entire cosmos be glad. Amen.

in churches. Such singing often is more robust, meaningful, and dialogic. The technology can help the community come alive in corporate praise to God. Now we need to reconsider other ways of using the various technologies to enhance the dialogue.

Much of worship is a kind of collective "naming" of reality under the authority of God and in the name of Jesus Christ. Singing, confessing our faith, preaching, reading Scripture, sharing communion, and the like all contribute to the dialogue of our collective liturgical naming done in thanks to God. We pray "in the name of Jesus Christ."

An acquaintance told me about a service he attended in which the pastor was welcoming the worshipers "in the name of—" when the Microsoft Windows logo came up on a screen behind him for the entire congregation to see. If that were not bad enough, the computer program then blasted the Windows boot-up sound over the house speakers. Instead of hearing the name of Jesus Christ, the congregation heard the Microsoft musical boot—a Star Wars–like welcome to the high-tech world of computing.

Liturgy helps us to order the dialogue, to make sure that the various voices speak, and to guarantee a time and place for the people of God to listen and then respond with praise and gratitude to the Creator's covenant with them. This is why, as I suggested earlier, liturgy is so important. Liturgy is not just for high-church folks; it is intrinsic to all worship. Liturgical actions are the very practices that transform our worship (and our lives) from chaos to cosmos. Just as God created the world out of chaos, our Creator's gift of faith engulfs us in gratitude and orients us to holy dialogue—all for the sake of directing us back into the world as agents of peace and justice. Psalm 33 reminds us to "let all the people of the world revere" God, for he spoke, "and it stood firm." The Lord "loves righteousness and justice."

Presentational technologies can be used well to facilitate worship as dialogue. They can show us what to read or see, whether we are reciting God's Word to us or our response to God. They can bring to our worship the voices and images of missionaries and homebound persons. Still and moving-image presentations are able to help us to see better who is reading or singing or preaching. Moreover, the process of creating presentations gives parish members an opportunity to construct the messages and artwork that will become part of the dialogue.

One additional point about the dialogue of worship is critical: as God has continued to speak in history, the church has recognized the texture of God's language, namely, the *story* of redemption. This story contains such events as the Israelites' freedom from bondage under Egypt, their liberation from exile in the desert, and the narrative reaches its climax when God sacrifices his only Son to guarantee believers' liberation from the burden of sin. In other words, God's speech within worship directs believers to remember and respond to the *narrative* promise of salvation. We can evaluate a congregation's use of presentational technology partly on the basis of how well it helps believers to retell, believe, and act upon God's true story of redemption.

We remind ourselves, as we listen to God's Word and to one another, that we are saved for service to God and neighbor. God's revelation, particularly through Holy Scripture, is that we are God's people and God is our God; we are called to respond gratefully to the promises of the Triune God to whom we owe every good thing. Liturgy is composed of the dialogic practices of collective remembering and responding. Worship is not meant to be a matter of simply distributing information, creating a spiritual high, or teaching a lesson. Corporate worship occurs as a group of faithful followers shares in the dialogue of life-changing communion with God, who authors the story of our salvation.

All Worship Is Multimedia

Worship has always been multimedia because human beings are multisensory creatures, not because of the existence of one or another human invention. We hear, see, touch, smell, and taste. In some traditions, most notably the Greek Orthodox, worship is tuned to all human senses in order to capture the fullest range of gratitude and praise among parishioners.[11] Clearly this is nothing new. Church historian Rebecca Lyman writes, "Whether viewing monks or holy sites, Christian piety of the imperial period [fourth and fifth centuries] was intensely physical. God had acted in human history, so the human senses were seen as aids to develop spiritual understanding."[12]

One liturgical scholar suggests that worship "depends upon our capabilities of sensing presence, of hearing, seeing, touching, moving, smelling, and tasting. . . . Christian worship is physically, socially, and culturally embodied." He also concludes that when worship appeals to all of the human senses—when it is truly multimedia—it is more likely to lead a congregation to the "essential qualities" of "awe, delight, truthfulness and hope."[13]

Today we are too inclined to forego older media in favor of newer ones. Let's not forget that we can reinvigorate past media while considering how to use more. Important media include liturgical pieces of art that drape the walls of many churches, the sanctuaries that provide space for worship, the sunlight and artificial light that focus worshipers' eyes within worship space, the physical contact worshipers have with the sacramental elements and with other believers (as in a greeting, passing the peace, blessing the children, or washing feet), the liturgical dancers who bodily enact our faith, the music worshipers hear, and the voices that sing to God in gratitude. Worship should indeed stimulate our imaginations in order to nurture our gratitude and deepen our praise. Any technological practice that can help us fulfill this God-ordained purpose is worthy of consideration.

Because worship is multimedia dialogue, liturgy and proclamation are nearly inseparable.[14] Liturgy includes reading of the Word, preaching from the Word, singing the Word, and enacting the Word in the sacraments. Liturgy offers many ways to dialogue through a host of God-given media. We read or sing God's own proclamations. We echo God's proclamations via banners, dance, songs, stained-glass windows, and computer screens. We try to echo, through all media at our disposal, the glory of God, the salvation of God's people, the sheer love of God for his creation in all of its manifold witness.

Is Your Worship Multimedia/Multisensory?

1. What appeals to sight?
2. What appeals to touch?
3. What appeals to the heart?
4. What appeals to the mind?
5. What appeals to smell?
6. What appeals to taste?
7. What appeals to hearing?
8. What appeals to you?

One church I visited a number of times recently has a pastor who is a remarkably gifted exegetical, expository preacher—he interprets and explains Scripture well. Many people attend the worship services solely to hear his sermons. He cogently illustrates the historical background of the selected biblical text with the help of a few projected images from art, architecture, maps, and the like. The pastor also uses screens fittingly to display Hebrew or Greek terms and to provide biblical references.

Nevertheless, his church's services lack multimedia dialogue. There is no greeting or benediction from God, in signage, in sanctuary art, or on the screen. There is no confession or forgiveness of sins. There is rarely a sacrament to see, smell, or touch. There is no intercessory prayer for the congregation, the community, and the world. On one church holy day, the service was silent about the church calendar. There is virtually no decoration of any kind in the sanctuary. After a few visits I concluded that the liturgy consists of singing praise to God and hearing a teaching from the Scriptures—"praise and preaching." On some days even the praise is missing; the liturgy consists of an hour-long sermon, like a lecture. People file in, sit down, listen, look, and file out. They are passive consumers.

Nonetheless, the preacher is a gifted biblical interpreter. He studies the biblical language, the historical context, and the ways various believers over the years have tried in commentaries to flesh out the application of the selected text to everyday life. His sermon lessons have a practicality that is lacking in many churches with richer liturgies. Clearly his preaching is the primary draw at this church.

In the end, however, it seemed to me that the presentational technology was not making the liturgy any richer. The screens and projectors failed to enhance the dialogue, except for singing. And the sad thing is that the technology was in place to do far more, especially in such a large church with many talented people. Just as in some low-tech churches, the liturgy offered few ways for God to speak to the people and even fewer ways for the people to respond gratefully to God in praise.

The Liturgical Elements of Worship

The Book of Hebrews addresses how our "vertical" dialogue with God informs the "horizontal" elements of our corporate worship. Hebrews highlights three responses of God's people to the gospel, namely, "drawing near to the Creator, holding to the hope that the community professes, and spurring one another on towards love and good deeds." Drawing near to God in public worship requires a public confession of sin coupled with an appeal for pardon and a prayer for strength to live godly lives. All of this is to occur in the context of the gospel of Jesus Christ, which is God's story for us as well as our story for living faithfully. David Peterson writes that "the praise of Christ for what he has accomplished, either in creedal form or in hymns and songs, will rightly be at the heart of the congregational meeting."[15]

For the early church such biblical themes established liturgical practices that still shape worship in most Christian traditions. These have included the reading of Scripture, commenting and reflecting on the reading, and publicly confessing or professing faith. By the third century the practice of the Eucharistic meal had become the major way of expressing Christian unity in the gospel of Jesus Christ. The Eucharist (Greek for "thanksgiving") was the shared *expression of* or even *participation in* the sacrifice of Jesus Christ, just as baptism took on a similar meaning for new converts, who through this sacrament "acted out" their dying to the old self and their rising in the new life of Christ (see especially Romans 6). The Eucharist was also called the Lord's Supper, love feast, Communion, memorial, and the breaking of bread.[16] All of these practices had biblical bases even though they were practiced somewhat differently by various Christian groups.

Important Liturgical Practices

1. Greeting or Invocation
2. Confession of Sins/Assurance of Pardon
3. Proclamation of the Word/Sermon
4. Public Prayer/Intercessory Prayer
5. Confession/Affirmation of Faith
6. Offering of Gifts and Lives in Service
7. Participating in Holy Communion/The Lord's Supper
8. Benediction/Blessing with a Charge to the Congregation

Worship planning, preparatory to using technology, requires a basic knowledge of the elements of liturgy. Although there are important and worthy differences across the various Christian traditions, there are also scriptural and historical continuities.[17] These *liturgical nonnegotiables* get at the heart of Christian faith as it is expressed in worship.[18] Although today we might assume that such nonnegotiables are stifling or old-fashioned, they still provide some elements of worship that can help us determine when we might use presentational technologies.

Worship typically begins with a *greeting from God* (or a welcome or an invocation), in whose name we meet. This practice sets the context for our public assembly as responsible agents of renewal who work and worship under God's authority. We belong to God, not to ourselves. We meet in response to his calling, not just at our own whim. God wishes to live in covenant with us. God therefore invites us to gather in the name of Jesus.

We will likely *confess our sins* together in order both to recall that God has forgiven us in Christ and to move closer to God in the intimacy of the cross. Confession is crucial for our ongoing sanctification. In worship, writes a theologian, "we not only in faith receive the word of forgiveness so freely spoken, but we receive it in repentance, submitting humbly to the guilty verdict (which is repentance) before the cross."[19] This is partly why so many Christian traditions ask believers to examine themselves and to confess their sins before partaking of the sacrament of Communion.

Clearly we should read from the Scriptures and *hear God's Holy Word*. Commenting upon the Word (which we now call "preaching") was one of the earliest practices in the church. Preaching the Word (or *proclamation*) is also a way of interpreting the text for a community of believers, so that the Scriptures are understandable and can be applied wisely to the lives of individual believers and the assembly. Reading the Word reminds us of the gospel as well as how we should live as a saved people. It instructs us in holy living, encourages and admonishes us.

Public prayer has been part of the corporate worship of Christians from the beginning. Prayer is a means for congregations to address God through Jesus Christ, who serves as our high priest and gives us direct access to the Creator. We pray both because God enjoins us to do so and because we know in our hearts, through the work of the Holy Spirit, that we need to seek communion directly with God, addressing him as a person, not as a remote, unapproachable deity. We know as well that God wants us to care about the brokenness of the world, just as Christ wept as he looked out over the city of Jerusalem before his death on the cross.

We ought also to *confess (or affirm) our faith* publicly as the early Christians did even in the face of persecution. Special practices such as adult baptism, confirmation of faith, and profession of faith are used for this task in various traditions. We should say that "Jesus is Lord" and believe in our hearts that God "raised him from the dead" (Rom. 10:9).

We *present our offerings* as a sacrificial expression of our gratitude to God, not merely to keep the church running as a social institution. God gives us all good things and sustains our lives daily. Just as the early church collected money for widows, orphans, and others, we contribute to the work of the church on behalf of people in need. The offering is symbolic as well as practical; it reminds us that we are called to give our entire lives to the Lord as a fragrant sacrifice.

Just as the *Lord's Supper* was the strongest expression of Christian unity in the early church, it remains vital to corporate worship "in the name of Jesus Christ." Believers understandably debate how or how often to celebrate the Eucharist, but its significance in the faith community is unequivocal. Christ instituted this sacrament on the night before he was hung on the cross at Calvary. Communion is one of the holy practices that Protestants and Roman Catholics alike take to be a sacrament. God calls us to "remember and believe" the sacrifice of Jesus Christ.

Finally, we should consider the importance of a concluding blessing or *benediction*, not merely to give the worship service unity but also to present the blessing, encouragement, and charge that we need to live out the gospel in the world outside the sanctuary. The benediction as blessing and charge says to us, "God has blessed you again. Now go into the world as stewards of God's creation and agents of redemption and renewal."

These eight important liturgical practices enable us as believers in Jesus Christ to share the "symbols and metaphors through which we talk about and make sense out of our world."[20] We can quibble about which of these practices is most crucial, how to order them in a service, what changes to make for seeker rather than believer services, and how to conduct them within the dialogue of worship. Frankly, I do not believe that any particular Christian tradition has perfected worship or ever will. Regardless of precisely how we conduct such practices, however, they help release us from the tight grip of the status quo.

Liturgy equips us to resist being worldly as we are conformed increasingly to the mind of Jesus Christ. We then are less inclined to be passive consumers of entertainment. To the extent that our liturgies merely replicate the practices and imaginations of the wider society (such as entertainment or teaching, where we become an audience or a class), they fail to furnish us with the shared vision and deep faith we need to be faithful disciples. Worship becomes a powerful style of life, an orientation to reality, even while the broken world mires us in sin.[21]

Finally, understanding these elements of Christian liturgy can give us insight into how we might use presentational technologies wisely to keep our worship both meaningful and biblical. How might we employ the various high- and low-tech media in the service of worshipful dialogue within each of these liturgical elements? Can we sing a confession? A profession of faith? Read together a psalm or another part of God's Word? Project an image during a greeting or benediction? What should we do visually during the Lord's Supper? By applying new technologies to age-old practices, a worship leader can help to enhance their significance for many worshipers.

Liturgy as Artistic Expression

One of the most surprising findings in our survey of more than eight hundred churches was that over half of them decided to begin using media technologies partly as a means of exploring another way of incorporating art into worship. Given the importance of art in worship, this is a wonderful opportunity.

Corporate worship is a public dialogue that ultimately serves as a fitting gift to God. Therefore, worship ought to be given well—both meaningfully offered from the heart and well created with the help of talented believers. Good liturgical art, whether music, dance, song, vestment, or banner, can enable us to perform more meaningfully and beautifully these elements of liturgy. Worship is meant to be artfully done, with respect for what is good, true, and beautiful—even what is pleasing to the senses. Worship is an offering *to* God while it is a dialogue *with* God and neighbor.

The *quality* of liturgy is just as important as its structure and integrity. Liturgical art does not need to meet the standards of any elite group. But we should pay attention to the artistic caliber of liturgy, which is one expression of gratitude to our Creator-Redeemer. Worship is meant to be a good gift, given well to the Creator who loved us before we even existed. In the Old Testament God gave the Israelites specific standards for building the tabernacle as a place for worshiping God (see Exodus 26). Our liturgical works still should be crafted with the talents that our Redeemer has poured out for us to enjoy and to offer back to God on behalf of the whole assembly.[22]

If we focus merely on the instrumental purposes of presentational technology—on merely the content of a message within the dialogue—we can lose track of artistic quality. Unfortunately, much of the liturgical use of presentational technology today is artistically substandard. The apparent power of technology to attract a congregation's attention and engage believers is proven every week in many churches. Such power should remind us, however, that we are responsible not only for the veracity of messages but also for the artistic *quality of the expression* of those messages.

A technology such as PowerPoint is so easy to use that it seems not to require much talent or giftedness. In a few minutes nearly anyone can compose a presentation of musical lyrics, scriptural readings, and sermon keynotes. But will the presentation be beautiful? Will it be good enough to be used throughout a church season or even from year to year on a given holy day? Some high-tech liturgical art is disposable after the service because there was so little heartfelt sacrifice in its design.

Evaluating Presentational Art

1. Is it beautiful?
2. Is it lovely?
3. Is it true?
4. Is it right and fitting?
5. Is it of excellent quality?
6. Is it worthy of being part of our praise of God?

—Adapted from Philippians 4:8

Nurturing Organic Community

Worship is also one of the main ways that Christians foster community. Here again, technology is crucial because it can become the "mediator" between worshipers. We worship *in* and *through* communication.

The New Testament concept of *koinonia* suggests far more than church organization. It means "community," "fellowship," and "participation." *Koinonia* is life together in the Spirit—serving each other as persons, not just offering formal church programs. The dialogue of worship provides many of the building blocks for communication within the church as community.[23] Worship directs us to participate as one in the divine life of Jesus Christ. We become the "body of Christ," an organism made up of self-sacrificial people who live together in communion with God and neighbor. Just as God gave his Son for our salvation, we serve each other.

We can assess the quality of our worship partly on the basis of how well it cultivates community. Is communication technology, in particular, helping us to get to know one another, serve one another, and love others? Are we better listeners and more deeply engaged in fellowship? Or does the technological scale and style of our worship transform the community into a gathering of tourists who merely pass by one another each week? Are we more than an audience? More than individual consumers of religious messages?

If we are not careful, our use of presentational technologies can become divisive. Used foolishly, they can divide congregations into markets or lifestyle groups, preventing communion across generations. This technology probably will not cause the same level of conflict witnessed in music-related "worship wars," but regardless, churches should move slowly, include the congregation in discussions about the use of technology, and seek uses that appeal to all generations.

The Spirit of Worship

Worship should be conducted in a spirit of reverence (God alone is entirely holy), gratitude (for all that God has done for us), and praise (simply because God deserves to be exalted for being God). Christian liturgy is partly a memorial that occurs in the presence of God. When our celebration takes on the tone of a concert, a classroom, or an office party, it lacks the reverence that it should have to be a humble offering to our Lord. When it lacks gratitude, worship can become self-satisfying for believers. Finally, when worship is deficient in praise, usually it is either too pedantic or merely entertaining.

This line between what is of the Spirit and what is not is sometimes difficult to discern. Every group that gathers for worship has to assess the spirit that drives its liturgical efforts. From pianos to PowerPoint, technologies often give power to particular persons or groups to enhance or demean the hearts of those who worship.

Human wisdom begins with the fear (or awe) of God. So should our worship. Worship is no place for a spirit of marketing, consumption, or entertainment, because then silence becomes uncomfortable. Stillness gives way to spectacle. The gift of spontaneous communion, surely a part of good worship, is no longer liturgically directed. The spirit of the age can eclipse the call to praise. Instead of listening to God and responding thankfully with praise, we start creating and responding to our own noisy racket.

Conclusion

When used well in worship, presentational technologies can enliven tradition and help to free some worshipers from meaningless traditionalism. *Traditionalism* is the "dead faith of the living," whereas *tradition* is the "living faith of the dead."[24]

We need tradition "as a guide and instructor, even as it seeks to give bona fide praise to God in a 'new song.'"[25] But we also need the Spirit. In recent decades some congregations have viewed technology as a means to "pump up" their services with impressive sights and sounds. Some of that technologically enhanced enthusiasm is probably a good thing. But technology itself cannot overcome meaningless traditionalism.

Presentational technologies can appropriately highlight sermon points and focus attention on particular liturgical practices. They can boost singing, provide worthy liturgical art, and offer many other benefits that I will discuss later.

When misapplied because of sloth, poor training, or a lack of understanding of worship, however, these same technologies can foster didactic teaching, inappropriate entertainment, or religious consumption to the detriment of worship. Understanding the meaning of liturgical elements and the flow of worship is crucial if we hope to practice corporate worship that is both biblical and meaningful.

3

Corporate Worship and Technology

> Whereas stained glass, vestments, banners, and baptistery art once created the sights of worship, now video projectors display fast-paced, syncopated images onto projection screens.[1]
>
> —Robert Phillips

Digital technology is simply a part of life for most people in industrialized societies. We depend on computers in automobiles, microwave ovens, and thermostats. Clocks keep us on schedule and divide time into ever smaller units. We fly on airplanes and trust scanners at the grocery store. A pastor told me recently about his granddaughter who puts videos in a VCR and plays the tapes—she is eighteen months old.

In our worship, too, we cannot escape technologies. Churches use heating and air conditioning systems, electrical lighting, pipe organs, and audio amplifiers.

Then there are the products of technology, such as books, furnishings, and liturgical implements (bowls, chalices, and candleholders). Someone probably has written a doctoral dissertation on the history of the various devices used to collect offerings. I read recently about a church that is accepting offerings via credit cards.

Technologies that have influenced worship historically include those related to biotechnology, information processing, sanitation, time keeping and astronomical instrumentation, and transport.[2] Technological innovations always have influenced corporate worship.

Some technologies are deeply embedded in liturgical actions, helping us to worship more meaningfully, beautifully, orderly, or effectively. For example, musical instruments facilitate the congregation in singing to the Lord.

Monastic worshipers devised timepieces as a means of regulating their daily worship "offices."[3] They probably had no idea that eventually most Christian liturgy in the Western world would be timed. The standard worship duration seems to be one hour even though this period is arbitrary.

The "Yes, But" of Wise Use of Technology

The problem of defining technology reminds me of Supreme Court Justice Potter Stewart's comment that although he could not define pornography, he knew it when he saw it. All of us think we can recognize technology—the lawnmower outside my office window, the car that just cruised by, the water guns that children in a neighbor's yard are using to keep cool on a warm July day, and a staple remover that is on my desk.

Gaining a deeper understanding of technology requires us to recognize and evaluate not just machinery but also our understanding of machines, including our notions of how to use them. This is the *rhetorical character* of our understanding of technology.

The ancient Greek idea of *techne*—the root word for technology—comes from the theory of "rhetoric" or "persuasion."[4] The Greeks recognized that words could influence individuals and society, even shape people's perceptions of reality. Using words well—powerfully, effectively, if not ethically—can persuade people. Just as electronic machines impact the world,

> **"Technology" Defined**
>
> Technology includes: (1) the *physical devices* (or tools) that we use to develop God's creation, (2) the *meanings* that we attach to these devices, and (3) the *ways* that we use them.

so do our sentences, artworks, novels, and films. Visual and verbal symbols, not just words, can alter our worship for good and bad.

The rhetorical aspect of technology demonstrates that devices can "mean" something to us. Technologies are powerful partly because they carry symbolic significance. Think of the automobile as a symbol of freedom or the television set as a symbol of personal entertainment. Today we define progress largely in terms of technological innovation and economic growth.

Communication technologies are not neutral tools that merely carry intended messages. Such devices often connote power, efficiency, and control—none of which is inherent in a physical device. Our technological practices shape how we perceive the world and hear others' words and messages.[5]

Technology, then, is made up of devices, meanings, and uses, all of which we apply to God's creation for various good and bad purposes. Generally speaking, the church does not create many new technologies. Moreover, the church is not the primary "definer" of the meaning of technology in society. Even my use of the word *creation* in the definition of technology (see above) is not an acceptable use in most books about technology. A creation implies a creator.

If a technology is a biased tool—if it includes particular meanings and practices—then we have to be careful about how, when, why, and where we use it. A wise approach to new technologies, then, is a "yes, but" attitude: *yes*, we will consider using it to serve our neighbors as ourselves, *but* we will not be duped by inflated rhetoric about its inherent goodness or badness. *Yes*, new technologies are part of the unfolding of God's original creation, *but* we fallen human beings will never be able to use them to usher in heaven on earth. The "yes" is our faith in God to bless our imperfect use of technology; the "but" is our admission of foolishness and hubris—all sin.

History shows that new technologies never live up to either utopian or apocalyptic rhetoric (remember Y2K?). Our answer to both technophiles and technophobes is "yes, but."

Four Approaches to Considering Technology for Worship

We have essentially three options when it comes to deciding what to do with technology in worship. First, we can *reject* a technology for a host of reasons. The financial costs might be excessive, especially in light of a congregation's commitments to missions, social justice, education, and more. Rejecting older or newer technologies can be a reasonable decision, especially if they will weaken worship or dissolve congregational fellowship or interfere with service to the community.

One of the major concerns that many congregations have is that presentational technologies automatically will transform worship into entertainment. This apprehension is rarely challenged because it seems so matter-of-fact. Film critic Neal Gabler writes, "The popular megachurch movement of the 1990s, which attracted thousands of worshipers to cavernous auditoriums, even implemented the same devices as any rock group trying to fill a stadium: not only the music but light shows and huge overhead projectors illustrating sermons or showing video clips. Some even had cappuccino carts and food courts."[6] Gabler's argument does not make it clear how the technologies necessarily contributed to the state of affairs that he describes. Many high-tech churches simply do not fall into Gabler's stereotype.

Nevertheless, we have to take possible problems seriously as we consider the role of presentational technologies in worship. And some congregations will find that particular technologies do not fit well with various modes, styles, or orders of worship. They might indeed discover that because of the worship tradition of their own congregation, projection screens do not foster better worship.

A second option is to *adopt* technologies—to bring them directly into worship. Adoption is the uncritical, unreflective practice of using new technologies *more or less as they are employed by people in nonliturgical settings*. We all know, for example, that audio amplification systems and microphones are used in many different ways in society, some of which may be appropriate for worship.

Many congregations acquire their ideas about how to use video clips and slides from outside the church. Two sources of external influence are business and education, where PowerPoint is largely a teaching technology for conveying bullets of information. It should not surprise us, then, that unreflectively adopting this kind of presentational technology sometimes leads a congregation toward a style of worship that increasingly emphasizes didactic instruction as the "delivery of information."

Four Approaches to Technology in Worship

1. *Rejection*—decide that there is no stewardly warrant for using particular technology in a worship style and tradition
2. *Adoption*—use technology in worship the way it is used for other purposes, such as teaching and entertainment
3. *Adaptation*—discern how, when, where, and why to use a particular technology appropriately in worship
4. *Creation*—invest in persons or organizations that will invent the next generation of technologies specifically for worship

The problem with adopting technologies from outside of worship is that usually we fail to consider their unintended impacts on liturgy. As Winston Churchill said of architecture, "We shape our buildings and afterwards our buildings shape us."[7] The same is true for all technological practices. As we adopt and institutionalize them, technologies generally modify how we think, feel, and communicate.

Churches are apt to adopt new technologies that symbolize power, which the church wants to use for good. One high-tech church speaks of the concept of "M to the Power of 3 . . . MultiCULTURAL, MultiSENSORY, MultiMEDIA." This was the title of a church's conference designed to teach participants from other flocks about "integrating media, environment and culture into your worship experiences creating spaces for life transformation."[8] An organization that promotes the use of cutting-edge technology in liturgy advocates "'the best' in technology to match the standards set by the entertainment industry."[9]

This kind of language about the power of media to influence people usually first surfaces in industry. One of the founders of the television channel MTV said during the channel's early years, "Our core audience is the television babies who grew up on TV and Rock & Roll. . . . The strongest appeal you can make . . . is emotionally. If you can get their emotions going, [make them] forget their logic, you've got 'em." He added that MTV's mood is "greater than the sum of its parts" and lauded the network for introducing programming that relies on "mood and emotion."[10]

The third approach to using technology in worship is *adaptation—wisely adapting new technologies to fit liturgical purposes*. This is a difficult way to proceed. It requires us to think carefully about the best ways to use communication technologies within worship for distinctly liturgical purposes. Once we put the purpose of worship ahead of the use of technology, we place demands on *when, how, where,* and especially *why* we use particular technologies. We cannot merely fall back on rhetoric about creating a "new visual language," "speaking to youth," or even "staying relevant." Instead, we have to justify the use of media within specific liturgical practices as *worship*. I advocate this approach.

The fourth approach to using technology in worship, *creation,* gives the church the most autonomy. Churches could support talented people and institutions in the development of technological innovations specifically for worship. In other words, rather than trying to adapt technologies from other contexts (like buying "secular" art for adorning church walls), congregations could become much more technologically proactive as patrons of liturgical art and presentational technologies. Unfortunately, the church today is not particularly interested in creating new technologies, although a growing number of liturgical artists are creating worthy material for worship.

Caretaking Liturgy for Shalom

The idea of technological adaptation brings us to the biblical basis for human use of technology, namely, our calling as caretakers or stewards of God's creation. Theologians sometimes speak of the "opening up" of God's creation as expressed in Genesis 1 and 2. God creates the world as "very good" and turns it over to humans to be its caretakers. We, too, are called to care for and develop this good creation—a *cultural mandate* echoed in the New Testament parables (e.g., Luke 19:11–27).

We "work" the creation nowadays, just as Adam and Eve began tilling the soil. God saves people not "*from* the world" but "*for* the world, to enable them to be his kings and priests ruling and redeeming creation."[11] In this sense, technological innovation per se needs no justification beyond God's own mandate for responsible human caretaking. We are to develop and use technology as stewards of God's creation.

Our vocation is based on responsibility, not exploitation. We are to use cultural-technological developments appropriately to serve our neighbors to the glory of the Creator. Regardless of how interesting or fun new technologies might seem to be, we are called to view them within this wider purpose of renewing a fallen world. Surely we can play with new gadgets that emerge from the unfolding of creation, but even play should serve the larger mission of bringing delight and fostering goodness.[12]

Perhaps the best term that we can use to understand our greater calling with respect to technological innovation is *shalom*. The word means something richer than keeping the Sabbath, namely, living in harmony with our Creator, with the creation, with other human beings, and with ourselves. Shalom signifies living obediently within God's commands rather than for our own interests and selfish desires. It directs us to human flourishing according to God's plan for our lives in a broken world. And it means, most fundamentally of all, that we become vessels of the grace of Jesus Christ, obedient disciples of the one who gave up his life for us. We are called to be carriers of love, agents of "peace and justice" in the world.[13]

Before we begin using new technologies in worship, then, we have to step back from the immediate practical problems—such as where to place projection screens and what kind of equipment to purchase—and consider first how technological practices will help to form us as caretakers of God's world and agents of shalom. We are not called to worship God merely to make ourselves feel better, to teach moral lessons, to learn about the Bible, to entice more people to worship, or to make a name for our church in the wider community. We are gospel-spreading and gospel-living caretakers. Worship can direct us to delight in God's world and to sacrificial lives of shalom-spreading gratitude. Our calling with respect to technology in worship is nothing less than to adapt humanly devised technologies to this good purpose.

Considering the New in the Context of the Old

With this view of biblical wisdom in mind, we can consider an important historical insight: *new "media forms" never replace older ones*. On the surface this claim seems at odds with our experience. After all, what happened to the hand-operated printing press or to the eight-track audiotape player? The rhetoric of technological progress gives us the false impression that the past is largely irrelevant to the present and that new human inventions always will render older ones obsolete.

When we look more closely, however, we discover that general *forms* of media never fully retire from human use, although earlier forms might be adapted to new practices. For example, the rise of printing did not replace speaking and listening, and electronic media have not eliminated reading and writing. God's creation is "opening up," not squelching everything from the past. Viewed in this context, the concept of technological progress is much more slippery than most people believe; the new does not completely replace the old. Only *particular technologies* disappear from culture, such as the rotary telephone or the feather pen, although some people will keep even these alive as collector's items or as a craft.

The unfolding of God's creation gives us the opportunity to adapt worship practices from church history—from the great "cloud of witnesses"—as well as from existing human culture anywhere in the world. We can use voice and microphone, press and projector, body and vestment, candle and spotlight. This is the real benefit of our high-tech era—the chance to use *all* of the media at our disposal, selecting wisely from the past as well as from contemporary life. We have a remarkable opportunity to use books, projectors, voices, and hands. We can learn about tradition as well as the present. We even can communicate with those of other traditions, selecting wisely from the broad range of media forms and communicative practices that have filled congregations' worship with praise throughout the ages.

Conclusion

When Saint Augustine became a follower of Jesus Christ, he faced a thorny situation: what to do with his rhetorical skills honed in the tradition of the Sophists, who were vendors of words for the sake of any cause. Augustine knew that such practices were simply not compatible with the responsibilities of Christians as caretakers of the truth.[14] For several hundred years before Augustine the church had given up on the art of rhetoric.

As Augustine grappled with this issue, however, he sensed the conflict between unreflective adoption and outright rejection of rhetoric. As a caretaker of the Word of God, Augustine correctly saw that persuasion was not inherently evil in spite of how some rhetoricians had perverted it. He also recognized that the salvation of souls does not justify all means of persuasion.

In faithfulness to God for his rhetorical inheritance, Augustine reclaimed rhetoric for the church, arguing that because Christians claimed God's truth, they had an obligation to advance that truth, to live it, to proclaim it in worship. He, too, was a sinner, but he lived in God's grace as a steward of creation and a caretaker of the church's legacy of truth telling.

Augustine's renewal of rhetoric gives us a model for how to think about technology today. Saying no to presentational technologies in worship, absolutely and for all time, is foolish. Yet to allow the sophists of our age—the people who seem to venerate technology for its power—to dictate how we approach presentational technologies in worship is just as wrongheaded. Utopian and dystopian talk about "high-tech worship" ought first to engage our defenses and next to remind us to recapture the purpose of worship in the fullness of God's unfolding creation. Then we might be wise enough to use new technologies (yes!) without falling prey (but!) to the rhetoric of our time that interprets every new communications medium as either the be-all or the end-all of humanly devised progress.

4

Avoiding Quick-Fix Techniques

> We ought not allow worship to be accommodated to current cultural norms to such an extent that worship loses its meaning.[1]
>
> —Robert E. Webber

We know from our survey of churches that nearly half of congregations intend to increase their use of computer projection systems. At the same time, however, one-quarter of the churches using the technology say that there would be no impact or only a slight impact if "the technology were removed" from their sanctuaries. If we add respondents who indicated there would be "somewhat" of an impact, we can account for about half of all surveyed churches.

What is holding these congregations back from making more effective use of presentational technologies? They say that money is by far the largest hindrance. About two-thirds of them would like more cash for improving their technology (see appendix).

This is a deeply held belief in America: money buys technology, which can improve just about everything.

Our gut sensibilities tell us that technological innovation is inherently good and that we should introduce improvements unwaveringly into every area of life. Commercials champion innovation as a sign of social and economic advancement. Our first response to the latest inventions is not a call to balanced assessment but rather to hop on the techno-train flying down the track.[2] The technological infrastructure all around us creates the intuition that there is a tool to solve every problem if we can only afford it.[3] Money procures progress; progress is good; churches ought to buy progress.

Instead of being a bit wary about the use of the latest technologies in worship, some churches acquire them like they are going out of style (and they are!). They set aside little time to assess older technologies because the new ones are already knocking on their sanctuary doors, looking for a temporary home. If earlier technologies did not quite live up to past expectations, we are not likely to care; we look to the future rather than to the past, where the reality of technological limitations is the clearest.

Our overly optimistic attitude toward using presentational technologies in worship reveals the quick-fix mentality of our times. No matter what the problem—medical, spiritual, economic, or political—we tend to assume there is an easy technological fix. Democracy needs online voting to boost voter turnout and accelerate the reporting of election returns. Curing cancer and other horrible diseases requires more money for research technologies. Education needs "smart classrooms." Business needs efficiency. We rarely talk about ethics, virtue, or even common sense. All we need is more technology and innovative techniques.

We cannot conquer our spiritual doldrums instantly with the latest powerful technologies. Moreover, God often reveals his glory by tabernacling among the weak.[4] The apparent power of technology seduces us into believing that we can eliminate everything that is arduous, difficult, and painful, when living for Christ calls us to self-sacrifice.[5]

In this chapter I evaluate some of the rationales that churches use to justify the use of presentational technologies in worship.

Eight Rationales for Using Presentational Technologies

1. *"We want to keep our young people interested in worship."* "We're losing our adolescents." "Our kids are bored with worship." "We need to make our worship experiences attractive to teens." "Adolescents grow up in an MTV world, and we need to compete if our church is going to survive."

These are the kinds of comments that I hear repeatedly from churches that are hoping to use presentational technologies to keep their youth in worship services. They are heartfelt responses to a real problem in many congregations and denominations. In our survey three-quarters of churches said they began using visual media technologies in worship to achieve "better relevance" for youth. The only higher percentage was for gaining "better relevance" for all members—including youth (see appendix).

But how do youth view the use of new technologies in worship? Here are the kinds of negative responses I have heard: "It's cheesy." "Compared to rock concerts, church is a joke." "Older people seem to like it." "If they are trying to keep us in church, why aren't we doing the media?"

Here are contrary responses from youth about using presentational technology in worship: "It's real." "This is worship for me." "I can invite my friends to church now."

Youth tend to be charitable but honest critics. Just ask them. Often they like high-tech worship but not if it is poorly done. And they wonder why adults make almost all of the decisions about worship style. They don't want to control worship. They just want adults to listen to them, too.

If churches are to compete technologically with popular culture, most of them are going to lose the battle. A few larger churches will spend up to several million dollars annually to approach the level of technical sophistication and visual and aural pizzazz evident in Hollywood blockbusters.

But who are we kidding when it comes to the average congregation keeping youth involved in church by importing flashy presentations into liturgical practices? Most of our productions will be second-rate compared with popular culture—unless we limit our efforts to what is appropriate for worship and what we can do well.

Possible Advantages to Using Screens for Singing

1. Churches can use music and lyrics from many sources.
2. Music leaders can adopt new music more quickly.
3. Worshipers are free to use their hands and bodies in singing.
4. Worshipers are more likely to look up and project their voices.
5. Visitors and others do not have to find the right books/pages.
6. It helps those who have difficulty holding a book/turning pages.

To the extent that presentational technologies are fitting for parts of your liturgy (more on this later), why not involve congregational youth in the planning, training, and use of such technologies? Some young people have skill and experience when it comes to designing computer graphics, editing videotapes, and using presentational software. Moreover, they frequently feel alienated from their church's liturgical practices. They might have some great ideas and be willing to employ their talents on behalf of the kingdom if your church can provide some solid mentoring. They could learn about liturgy in the process. One of the strengths of high-tech churches is that they tend to be more open to the gifts and talents of younger members.

2. *It's time to boost the quality of congregational singing.* Contemporary worship music is melody driven and relatively easy to sing. Because most of the songbooks in use do not include such music, worship leaders employ overheads and other means of projecting lyrics on a screen. I have heard repeatedly from advocates that this music, when projected on a screen, stimulates congregations to sing vibrantly. So far this probably has been the greatest benefit of using presentational technologies in worship.

Nevertheless, the real value of this technological and musical innovation occurs when congregations modify their liturgies over time to attract more outwardly emotional worshipers. Much worship in America is unemotional partly because it addresses the mind much more than the heart. Praise music addresses this felt need for many people.

If the rest of the liturgy is untouched, however, will members sing more enthusiastically just because words are on a screen and hands are free to be raised? Not always, because each congregation has its own, long-existing culture influenced by ethnicity, neighborhood, age, and the like.

When my wife and I were in Florida on sabbatical, we visited a number of congregations that had introduced praise bands and projected lyrics within an existing church culture that could not sustain the modification. The result was awkwardness in worship. People seemed to want to lift up their hands, but hardly anyone did. The dissonance between the style of the music and the congregational response made us feel badly for the praise singers, who themselves seemed to be uncomfortable about the situation.

Possible Disadvantages to Using Screens for Singing

1. It might over time weaken harmonic singing.
2. Many young people will not learn how to read music.
3. Parents can't follow the music with their fingers for young children.
4. The visually impaired will still need large-print books.
5. Screens detract from the beauty of the sanctuary.
6. Learning a new song is more difficult.

There are vibrant traditions of singing with printed music—traditions that some churches might do well to revive rather than trying to imitate other churches. In the past many congregations taught themselves to hold their hymnals high, raise their heads, and project their voices. Technological changes will not automatically revive these practices. Maybe nothing will in some congregations.

Moreover, we ought not to allow congregations to become musically illiterate by singing only melodies and without music scores. Historically speaking, churches often were the main venue for composers, musicians, and vocalists to hone their musical talents. The church serves society, not just itself, by continuing to use some music that requires more than reading simple lyrics.

Fortunately companies sell programs that enable churches to project music as well as lyrics on the screen. And in some cases, congregations are ready spiritually and culturally for new song lyrics projected this way. We should use new music when it is doctrinally sound, leads people to praise God, and helps to form the parishioners into God's obedient people.[6]

3. *We need to change with the culture or we will lose members to other churches.* It's time to embrace the twenty-first century, or so the argument goes. Churches that fail to adopt new worship technologies will become dinosaurs, extraneous to the broader culture. High-tech is the future, whether we like it or not.

Since some people prefer worship that includes more technology, this is probably a legitimate concern. Nevertheless, each congregation has to discover its route to faithfulness, given its distinctive history, local community, and available gifts and talents. The twenty-first century will not look the same for all congregations. Nor should it. Liturgical diversity is a sign of spiritual vibrancy.

One contrary cultural trend is worth considering for the sake of balance. A growing number of people who live high-tech lives at work seem to be opting for simpler lifestyles at home and leisure.[7] Perhaps the twenty-first century will also be a time of low-tech churches. Rather than simply lurching into extensive use of technology in worship, congregations should consider how best to serve their members and neighborhoods. Technology might or might not be helpful, depending on the situation.

One Seattle pastor has decided to go low-tech even though half of his church works at Microsoft. Looking at the quality of so much video, DVD, film, and computer production, he decided not to "try and keep up. So, we go stripped down laid back and first century. I'd rather do spoken word poetry, dance, silence, meditation, readings, and about an hour-long narrative theology sermon than lots of glitz."[8] He rightly looked at his own congregation and decided that they needed worship with less technology.

4. *We have to create more powerful worship experiences.* For whatever reasons—and surely there are lots of them—many people do not feel the presence of God or the fellowship of the faithful in worship. "Going to church" for them is an empty ritual at best and merely a means of staving off guilt at worst.

One of the reasons for this situation is that more and more people do not have the time to engage in spiritual disciplines that would help the faith come alive for them and for their parishes. Personal prayer, Sabbath keeping, hospitality, personal and family devotions, contemplation, Bible reading and study, small-group involvement, catechism classes, Sunday school, and many other practices are important for the health of corporate worship, not just for the spiritual lives of individual members. Weekly worship can hardly take on the burden of meeting a congregation's spiritual needs.

Moreover, an overly enthusiastic desire to use technology to create a powerful worship experience can too easily lead a church to a darkly utilitarian view of worship. Simplistic ends—like an emotional high or a feel-good experience—do not justify technological means.

Worship has become heavy-handed in some high-tech worship settings.[9] A colleague recently attended a media-saturated service that she described as too visually manipulative and aurally inundating to nurture godly worship. The service was largely a show—a multimedia extravaganza, with no time for silence and contemplation. As soon as the service was over, worshipers flew out the doors without looking back. Within minutes my colleague was one of the only people left in the building.

Liturgy can be reduced to engineering maximum impact on audiences. This mechanistic concept assumes that worship should be like a machine, calculated and packaged to meet spiritual and religious needs.[10]

Perhaps the issue is whether or not we should think of worship in terms of how well it holds people's attention and relieves their boredom. "I love movies," says one pastor who uses video clips in worship. "If a picture is worth a thousand words, then a video has to be worth a million."[11] But worship is not primarily about powerful or poignant feelings. It is about thankfully praising God and renewing faith for service. Worship is not meant to hinge on individual or collective experience but to focus our attention on what God has done, is doing, and has promised to do in the world. Ultimately, liturgy is the work of God's grace in our lives, not our techniques for creating experiences.

5. *We want to let visitors and members know that we are a first-rate church.* This rationale rightly suggests that believers ought to attend to the impression that their worship facilities, services, and technologies give to the wider world.

What concerns me, however, is the way that giving a good impression can become an argument for meeting the world's standards. Congregations surely need to aim higher than conspicuous consumption of technology. But the idea of "keeping pace" (dare I say "being competitive") with other churches is hardly virtuous in and of itself. Yet over one-third of our survey respondents said that "keeping pace with other churches" was one of the reasons that they began using media technologies in worship.

What about parishes that like to talk about vast new auditoriums, state-of-the-art video control rooms, and stadium-quality projectors? Is this pride or thankfulness to God? Some impressive high-tech congregations are faithful stewards of what God has entrusted to them even if they become a bit prideful. Both low-tech and high-tech churches can be boastful. There is plenty of bluster to go around.

Yet the tales of high-tech church progress can be particularly thin, lacking a concern for good stewardship. A goal of being first-rate technologically, without a commitment to worship per se, is not a sign of godly progress. If a church brags about its investment in presentational technologies, but its presentations could be done almost as well with hundreds of thousands of dollars less, something is fundamentally wrong. This is indeed the case in some churches.

Why not impress people with the *quality* of worship and the *richness* of congregational life—with or without high-tech methods?

6. *Without using new technologies, we will not be able to increase the size of our congregation.* Our survey found that about two-thirds of all churches in the country began using media technologies in worship at least partly in order to gain "seeker sensitivity."

This is a knotty rationale to address, however, because larger, wealthy congregations often have all kinds of other things going for them: greater word of mouth (the best church "advertising" there is), higher visibility locations (usually along suburban highways), plenty of parking, a less threatening environment because of being able to visit anonymously, a larger and more skilled technology staff, paid worship leaders and sometimes even musicians, psychological momentum, and more. Smaller churches are not as likely to use advanced technologies well, partly because they do not have the resources or expertise and partly because they sometimes overestimate their own capabilities.

Numerical congregational growth is a thorny criterion. Depending on what else comes with it, it could be blessing or bane to good worship.

7. *Presentational technologies will allow us to expand our worship space.* This rationale carries considerable weight because all churches should consider the visual and aural aspects of worship space when they move to a new sanctuary or restore an existing one. If a church is growing numerically, a time will come when its existing worship space will not be adequate. The congregation could decide to launch a daughter church, but in any case it should not enlarge the sanctuary without considering the impact on worship.

Both traditional pews and the newer theatrical seating can hamper liturgical practices. Because worship involves the use of the body, we should consider the physical flexibility of liturgical space. If worshipers are only standing up and sitting down nearly any space can function well. But if the space has to serve a number of other actions, such as coming forward for prayer, anointing members, laying on of hands, serving Communion in groups rather than individually, and kneeling, the members will have to consider complex issues associated with spatial expansion. Limited-purpose settings are always easier to design when it comes to presentational technologies. This is partly why so many newer church buildings are essentially auditoriums.

My comments about this issue undoubtedly are influenced by my view of congregational life as "communion." It is more difficult, but not impossible, for large congregations to function very well as communities unless they foster small groups or other relational ministries. Technology can expand the spatial scale of worship with enhanced visual and aural clarity, but technologies cannot guarantee that congregants will *be* a church, only that they can *do* church. Regardless of how much presentational technology a congregation implements, a church has to use the technology to counter mainstream culture, which defines public events in terms of *consumption* rather than *participation*.

8. *New technologies offer us a means of serving members of our congregations who are hard of hearing or have difficulty seeing.* This alone is a solid argument in favor of incorporating presentational technology in worship.

One of the mistaken assumptions about presentational technologies is that older members of a congregation will not like them. One church that I attended is filled with senior citizens during the winter. Volunteers project sermon points and song lyrics on a large screen in the front of the redesigned sanctuary. Participants who want to use the hymnals in the pews can do so, but those who find it difficult to turn the pages in a book or to read the print in the hymnals have the option of following the text on a screen. This church also respects harmonious singing by including as appropriate the music with the lyrics on the screen. The place where the screen is hung is dark enough and the font type is large enough that the words can be read easily from anywhere in the relatively large sanctuary.

As followers of Jesus Christ we need to think seriously about how new technologies can serve those in our churches who have special needs. To bring them more fully into corporate worship is a laudatory goal. It is one thing to improve only marginally the quality of worship for everyone in a congregation and something far greater to include in the liturgical dialogue people who are otherwise unable to participate well or fully.

Worship as Worship

Authentic worship has intrinsic value apart from the ways we try to manufacture worship experiences. All leisure (including worship) is meaningful in itself. Praising God is intrinsically right and good. As Josef Pieper put it in *Leisure: The Basis for Culture,* "'We praise you, we glorify you, we give you thanks for your great glory.' How can that ever be understood in the categories of rational usefulness and efficiency?"[12]

In the hope of producing the ultimate worship experience, we can unknowingly transform our liturgical actions into mere technique. We then subject worship to *utility*—what *we* can accomplish through *our* effort. Such a technical view of worship can lead a congregation to self-engineer liturgy rather than to worship for God's own sake.

Even music can become a mere technique for inducing a particular response. "Those who truly *want* to worship, *as an ongoing condition of the heart,*" says a scholar of music, "should not credit music with the power to bring worship about. They will worship irrespective of music."[13] Indeed, such faithful people will worship irrespective of any technique or technology. Our Lord is sovereign, but we are called to be responsible coworkers. To squash the Spirit in our liturgy is to focus on "calculation and control" and "exclude grace and surrender."[14]

Right and fitting worship must avoid the "twin evils of control and chaos." Some churches like "having everything nailed down into place so that the Spirit is effectively locked out, and others—like the Corinthians in 1 Corinthians 14—so spontaneous and ill-disciplined as to threaten the gospel by their structure as much as their content."[15] Being "inspired" in worship is not enough. When Christians gather to worship, the practices "should convey meaningful truth."[16] They should bind the assembly together with Christ by the power of the Holy Spirit. Perhaps the resulting gratitude is the best measure of authentic worship. To be grateful to God and to give praise are bedrocks of real worship in the Spirit.

Conclusion

I hope that my warnings in this chapter are legitimate causes for concern about the headlong rush to implement novel technologies. The quick-fix mentality is not merely a reflection of our broader cultural biases toward self-help techniques and greater efficiency and control. At root the mentality reflects a human tendency to idolize technology. It shifts our perspective from how to discern good and fitting worship to how to accomplish various instrumental purposes that may or may not be fragrant offerings to our Lord.

We already see in North America pockets of "technologized" worship that are not fitting. Celebrity preachers and worship extravaganzas are just two of the more obvious manifestations of this problem. Worship should direct our attention to God rather than to our own efforts. The work of liturgy is not meant to impress anyone but rather to reflect the grace of God in our midst. "Most important," says one writer, "our churches must give up the superstitious belief that quick techniques can offer solutions to the intractable problems of being Church in a non-Church society."[17]

5

Fitting Technology into Worship

The choice today is not "between Mozart and the Internet," but between what is sensible and what is not.[1]

—Nathan Mitchell

Wisdom should compel us to use presentational technologies within the context of worship—not to use worship to celebrate technology. There is no such thing as purely "high-tech worship" any more than there is "no-tech worship." Worship is worship, and it is intrinsically good when liturgical practices respect scriptural integrity and take into account proven worship traditions. Today we suffer not just from a penchant for liturgical quick fixes but also from an ignorance of the practices that churches have used through the ages to foster fitting worship.

In this chapter I address the *fittingness* of technology with good worship.[2] I could have used terms such as *congruence, suitability,* or *appropriateness,* but to me fittingness better connotes a sense of rightness, integrity, and orderliness. I am concerned with the *fit* within some *givens* of good worship and within a particular liturgical movement or tradition. Paul reminds us that God is a God of order and peace, and everything in worship should be done in a "fitting and orderly way" (1 Cor. 14:33, 40).

Liturgical Fittingness

Fittingness suggests that we employ presentational technologies *in the service of the liturgy*. Rather than worshiping technique or technological devices, we endeavor to worship God. Nicholas Wolterstorff helpfully suggests three aspects of liturgical fittingness that we can apply to presentational technologies.

First, digital presentations should be performed with *clarity*. If they obscure what God is saying or how the congregation should be responding, they interfere with the dialogue of worship. Simple, direct communication is nearly always better than a projected message that includes too much information or too many different images.

Second, liturgical actions should not *distract* congregants from the worship itself, drawing attention to the presentations rather than to the flow and meaning of the liturgy. A minister friend says that computer presentations almost always are better than the work of "bumble-fingered overhead attendants." He has a point. Done well, digital presentations are much more seamless and less disruptive than old-fashioned overhead projections.

I once attended a church where the animated texts, flying onto the screen to illustrate sermon points, elicited so much attention that some worshipers were jabbing those seated next to them with great delight, as if to say, "Wow, is this technology great!" Both the animated text and the response of the congregation to the flying words distracted us from worship.

Third, liturgical practices should not create any undue *awkwardness* or *difficulty*. This can cause trouble partly because presentational technologies typically involve numerous people in planning and conducting worship. When a church first adapts presentational technologies to worship, it needs a bit of time for the congregation, the technologists, and the worship leaders to become comfortable with the innovations.

In this chapter I will broaden the discussion of fittingness to include additional dimensions. I suggest that *we need to consider the fittingness of presentational technologies for particular liturgical practices and within the broader context of a liturgical movement or tradition*. Established congregations usually inherit liturgical practices that might be worthy of preserving. A wise congregation will adapt presentational technologies to proven practices.

Three Potential Problems in Worship Presentations

1. Lack of clarity
2. Distraction from worship
3. Awkwardness or difficulty in presentation

The idea of "one size fits all" or, as they say in high-tech culture, a "turnkey solution," makes no sense in the context of worship. We ought to be creative and flexible in our worship planning but without discarding the valuable practices instituted by earlier generations of worshipers. Fittingness has theological and historical as well as contemporary and practical components.

Who is to say that Free Methodist or Missouri Synod Lutheran or Independent Baptist worship should be the same technologically? Or that two Episcopal or Roman Catholic churches in the same city, each with its own history and congregation, should employ technologies identically? Would not such sameness suggest a bowing down to the urgency of the present and disrespect for the particularities of tradition and local practices? Yet this is precisely the problem we face with the rapid adoption of presentational technologies; many congregations want to copy how other churches use them.

A desire for fittingness should lead us to consider at least the following: (1) worship season, (2) type of service, (3) architecture and worship space, (4) artistic and aesthetic considerations, (5) place in the order of worship, and (6) theological-liturgical tradition/movement.

Worship Seasons

Throughout church history the worship seasons have been important in establishing liturgical practices. Some churches

Causes of Presentational Distraction and Awkwardness

1. Text is unreadable from a distance
2. The meaning of images does not fit with the meaning of text
3. Slides appear in the wrong order
4. The timing of the presentation does not match where the congregation is reading, singing, or reflecting
5. Jumpy transitions from slide to slide
6. Lack of aesthetic unity across all slides in a presentation

still follow a yearly calendar, celebrating seasons such as Advent, Epiphany, Lent, Easter, Pentecost, and Trinity. Seasons can "become a root of Christian life . . . when they draw us into the story of God, implicating us into the future of peace and healing that is already breaking into the present time."[3] All congregations participate in the church calendar, however muted.

What about the suitability of high-tech practices within the church season? Is Good Friday as fitting as Easter? Which holy days should be more silent and pensive? Easter has been the great celebrative day of the church through many centuries, followed in significance by Pentecost—a season that attends to the power of God through the Holy Spirit that surely ought to be filled with wonder, delight, and mystery. A low-tech, exceedingly simple, and perhaps even stark service on Good Friday could reasonably be followed by a fully celebrative and multimedia service on Easter.

Type of Service

One congregation in my area maintains a traditional Presbyterian liturgy but uses presentation technologies very well in two special services every year. The downside of this approach is that the planning committee has to pull together appropriate technology just for these two services. The upside is that the church does those two high-tech services very well. The worship committee vigilantly plans them, asking the right questions about doing presentation technologies well, with much attention to detail.

Apart from the season, congregations plan many types of services, such as those for baptism, testimony, confession or profession of faith, prayer, memorial, and healing. Often such services are accentuated with a special liturgy. Presentational technologies provide creative opportunities beyond weekly Lord's Day worship.

In planning every service we should be aware of possibilities and mindful of potential problems related to clarity, distraction, and awkwardness. I have been impressed with visual presentations of the lives of adults who are making public professions of faith; particularly in larger churches, it is difficult to know these people personally, and even a simple presentation with a few slides and comments from the new believer can both inform the congregation and encourage members in their own spiritual journeys. Similarly, I have witnessed some splendid reports about the work of church youth groups in mission fields, followed by services of thanks for the young people's safety and a petition to God to bless the ongoing work of believers still in the field. Some congregations use slides or video to display close-ups of babies or adults who are being baptized.

Architecture and Worship Space

This is a hornet's nest of differing opinions. I tread lightly, asking some decisive questions rather than pretending that I have all the answers about how to use worship space to the glory of God.

Most of us worship in spaces that were not designed for presentational technologies. Often we lack appropriate wall space for projection screens or secure places to mount projectors. In a few churches the level of sunlight entering the front of the sanctuary makes it necessary to use high-power projectors; to block the entering light either would be too difficult or could ruin the aesthetics of the windows and the worship space.

Following the lead of the great cathedrals, many church buildings have long sanctuaries with only moderate natural light from elevated windows. Depending on the orientation of the windows to the south, the room might be dark enough for projection with-

Positioning a Screen in a Sanctuary

1. What are the architectural and decorative nonnegotiables that you must work around—art, lighting, organ pipes, congregational visibility, etc.?
2. Which spaces are clear and free in the center or on the sides of the front of the sanctuary?
3. Must the screen be hung permanently, or could you use a motorized screen, which is heavier, costlier, and requires power?
4. What is the angle of viewing for those in the front rows of the sanctuary (keeping in mind that anything over thirty degrees will cause neck pain)?
5. Where could the projector(s) be mounted, considering the screen location, power, and transmission line requirements?

out any modifications. In other cases, especially with modern architecture, shading the windows might be necessary. One advocate of presentational technologies even suggests, "If budget is a concern, and your worship space is just too bright, consider going to an evening service when daylight is not a factor."[4] That seems a bit extreme to me.

Redesigning existing churches for presentational suitability is becoming a noteworthy architectural specialty, although architects and liturgical planners do not always agree about how to plan such alterations. Creative architects seem to be able to adapt new technologies fairly seamlessly to the original building design.

We ought to have reservations about the concept of refashioning our worship space solely for the ease of high-tech worship—without considering how the space will facilitate liturgy. Presentational technology should not dictate *where* or *when* we worship any more than *how* we worship.

Our liturgical practices occur in two God-given dimensions, time and space. Time relates not just to the timing of the parts of liturgy but also to the relationship between our worship and God's redemptive acts in history. Worship traditions include liturgical concepts that enable a group of believers to participate in shared practices such as singing, celebrating the Lord's Supper, and hearing testimonies of faith. Learning how to worship within a tradition is a means of building continuity with the past; the best architecture equips us to do this well.

How we use space for liturgy says much about our theological convictions. In fact, all architectural design carries with it an implicit theology of worship. For a congregation that sees itself as an "army of God," the basilica shape is appropriate. A parish that views itself as "God in the world" might prefer the form of a tent.[5] Probably the most important issue is how the worshipers relate spatially to God, to each other, and to the rest of the world. Does the space suggest the "priesthood of all believers" or "God the high priest"? Does the room treat worship leaders and soloists as directors and leaders, or does it position them as equal members of the congregation? I have simplified the issue of liturgical space only to suggest that technological placement ought not to be the most critical factor.

Probably the best situation is adapting an existing worship space to new technology rather than letting the demands of the technology determine how worship space is designed. I do not prefer worshiping in space that seems like an auditorium rather than a church. Nor do I like worship space that is dominated visually by a screen. Nevertheless, I recognize that sanctuary design is a matter of taste as well as theology and church governance.

Not all existing worship spaces can be adapted well to presentational technologies without a substantial financial investment. Clearly this is a stewardship issue that each church has to face if it decides to use presentational technologies regularly. A congregation easily can spend several hundred thousand dollars just on redesigning a sanctuary.

Aesthetic Considerations

We are created by God to flourish in beautiful environments. As the creation itself makes clear, God does not intend for us to dwell in ugliness. We can glorify God by skillfully adorning our worship areas. Fitting worship is artistically appropriate and aesthetically inspiring. The place where we worship should lead us to lift up our hearts to the Lord.

Adorning a worship space with human works of beauty is not poor stewardship unless a congregation is spending outrageous sums on fine art or on special commissions that are out of tune with the flock's overall budget and the needs of the wider community. Adornments can include banners, paintings, sculpture, and special displays. Stained-glass windows and appropriate interior decorating are important in many traditions. Sacramental furnishings can convey liturgically appropriate beauty as well. Some traditions are more austere than others, but the basic principles of artistic design still apply; elegance can be simple as well as stylish.

Presentational technology is another medium for beautifying our worship settings. Ironically, few congregations seize this opportunity because they generally view technology narrowly as a means for conveying information—from bulletin announcements to sermon outlines and song lyrics. New technologies ought to be considered a means of developing "liturgical media art."[6] To grasp some of this aesthetic potential, however, we have to recognize that liturgical art need not be preachy.

Like a simple but graceful banner that might not contain words, a video or slide projection can help establish the right setting for worship. Presentations also can contribute to a particular theme of worship on a given day, a church season, or a special service. Projections can help dress the sanctuary for fitting liturgical practices.

The Internet has become a hindrance as well as a help in developing presentational art. It is so effortless to download aesthetically inferior images and paste them quickly into a computer presentation that some church services are beginning to look like comic pages or clip-art collages. Today we have to resist the temptation to snatch images online at the last minute to add visual interest to text presentations during sermons and songs.

Presentations need not be elite art. Simple but appropriate beauty is enough. The artistic quality of presentations is just as important as their instructional value; an instrumentalist view of presentational art as message can rob us of an aesthetically fitting means of glorifying God. God deserves the best, including the best presentational art.

Place in the Order of Worship

Another consideration for the fitting use of presentational technologies is their place in the order of worship—the sequencing of liturgical actions. Worship services normally begin and end a particular way, and congregational prayers and sacraments likely occur in order between other liturgical practices. The Scriptures call for worship to be done in good order (1 Cor. 14:40), so we ought to arrange the elements of worship according to a liturgy and on the basis of what works well for a particular congregation.

What is a fitting presentation during the Lord's Supper? Should the elements of Communion be the visual focal point? If so, should such images be projected on a screen or should the congregation be encouraged to look directly at the bread and wine or juice? The use of projection during sacraments can distract worshipers from the liturgy or lead them into deeper contemplation, depending on how it is integrated with the liturgy.

Congregational announcements represent a similar dilemma. Some churches project announcements immediately before the service begins while others do so at the end of the service or during the offering. I prefer liturgical art on the screen before the service to help me prepare my heart and mind for worship. But I know from conversations with people from various liturgical traditions that my preferences do not match many others' desires.

Common Uses of Presentational Technologies

1. Establishing preservice mood
2. Providing preservice information (e.g., prayer needs, events)
3. Building congregational anticipation
4. Creating congregational identity/image (e.g., a logo or theme)
5. Facilitating singing, song leading, and performance
6. Showing the sacraments
7. Supporting the children's lesson
8. Monitoring the service remotely (e.g., in narthex)
9. Projecting video clips, music videos, and promotional videos
10. Displaying Scripture or page numbers
11. Visually illustrating sermon ideas/text background
12. Providing a sermon outline
13. Reinforcing a sermon theme with visual symbols

I have been impressed with how well some pastors use projected "visual aids" during sermons. People do tend to remember better visually. Some pastors already have become adept at using projected images to illustrate the cultural and social background of the biblical text. Pastors show such things as the idols that apostate groups worshiped in biblical times, the shores of the Dead Sea, and the Roman armor that Saint Paul associated with God's protection. Preaching ought not to be reduced to a didactic slide show or a video excursion, but a few well-selected images can give additional vitality and relevance to a sermon or homily.

Some churches project popular commercials and film clips in order to make sermon points more immediately relevant. This approach appeals to many worshipers who seek to know how their faith should relate to contemporary popular culture. Once again the issue is whether or not such use of projection is fitting to the purpose of worship. Are video clips designed to create a fashionable church ethos? Are they used to lure people into the church? Are they entertaining and fun for the congregation, especially young members? What is their worthy purpose?

I spoke recently with a mother who told me she was banning her teenage daughter from a church that projected video clips of popular movies during sermons. This sincere parent was concerned that the culturally pertinent sermons were directing her daughter to popular culture rather than to a disciplined life of faith. I could see her point, but I also wondered if the mother was being realistic; her adolescent probably was going to view movies regardless of whether parts of them were projected during worship.

Fittingness requires video clips to be an accepted part of the style and substance of the pastor's proclamation within a given congregation. In some churches these clips can help to furnish the congregants with a prophetic perspective on the world outside the sanctuary.

The Importance of Liturgical Traditions/Movements

Recently I spoke at a seminar on using technology in worship. I raised this question to spur discussion about the differences among liturgical traditions: "Could you imagine good worship without a pipe organ?" One senior woman in the front row immediately shouted at me, "Absolutely not." She even waved her hand at me dismissively as if to say, "Who is this guy, anyway?" In response I asked the group how we should think about worship before the invention of the organ. Was previous worship invalid or less pleasing to God? I asked about stewardship as well because the pipe organ still is the most significant technological expense for a congregation.[7]

No one had a quick response to that question, so I probed a bit deeper: "What do you think about the noninstrumental Christian traditions?" Some listeners looked at me like I was from Mars. They wanted to know what I meant by "noninstrumental"—no instruments whatsoever? The idea of such a tradition seemed absolutely alien to them. No one in that group was willing to embrace the notion that even today we might discover some liturgical *strengths* in a noninstrumental tradition.

Understanding liturgical traditions is probably the most important means of discerning the fittingness of presentational technologies in worship. When I am out of town I like worshiping in churches from different traditions. The experience helps me to comprehend and value the ways that various Christian groups worship. No Christian tradition can lay claim to liturgical perfection. As one worship historian puts it, "Even when we speak of 'apostolic tradition'—the teachings of Jesus that were preached through the earliest missionaries or apostles—we are talking not of a single uniform formula, but a collection of beliefs and practices. It is a coherent and recognizable collection, but it is not monolithic."[8]

Liturgical traditions and more recent liturgical movements can learn from each other even as they respect their own, distinct integrity. Newer, seeker-oriented churches can benefit by reacquainting themselves with historic liturgical practices. Older congregations can learn much from seeker services, including about how to use presentational technologies well.

In recent years liturgical renewal has taken the form of "movements" that are less tightly tied to specific worship traditions. Robb Redman, author of *The Great Worship Awakening,* identifies four important worship movements today: (1) the seeker service movement, (2) the praise and worship movement, (3) the contemporary worship music industry, and (4) the liturgical renewal movement.[9] These categories can help some churches identify where they are on the liturgical renewal spectrum.

We ought to consider how each of our liturgical traditions and movements might fit with presentational technologies. What are the liturgical strengths of how we worship? Do we have a clear enough sense of our congregational and denominational self-identities that we can even make such judgments?

Understanding Our Own Tradition

A congregation must understand its own liturgical practices if it hopes to assess opportunities for using presentational art and text. To ignore such fundamental understandings is to risk becoming a nondescript church with a liturgy of convenience or instrumental imperatives.

A church that is aware of its liturgical tradition will be better equipped to adapt presentational technologies in a way that respects tradition but is open to opportunities to practice worship even more fittingly. Rather than merely imitating the deeply ingrained media routines that we acquire from the wider culture—from mindless film watching to frenetic TV-channel switching—we need to ensure that our presentations fit the purposes of good liturgical order and connect with our congregation's own, local cultural setting.

My adopted tradition contributed historically to harmonious singing of hymns and especially the psalms (metrical psalmody). If that is a good and fitting liturgical practice—John Calvin thought that singing psalms put God's words into the mouths of congregants—then my church ought to keep that practice alive both for itself and for other churches and traditions that might want to adapt the practice. Of course the psalms can be adapted to new, even melodious music, but some of the previous adaptations ought to be maintained as well. Their influence in edifying believers for hundreds of years is indisputable.[10]

Local differences in liturgical fittingness are important, too. I received a note recently from a woman who organizes the visual presentations at a church near Columbine High School, the site of the tragic shootings in 1999. "My church has students, teachers, etc., who attended Columbine," she wrote, "and so I know that whenever I use an image that has that flower in it, it may have an impact on someone in the congregation that's not related to the song at all." She is rightly sensitive to the particular visual associations that her congregation will make with images that worshipers in other locations might find wholly suitable.

Liturgical traditions, always anchored to a local context, center our worship, give it particular shape and substance, and frame it stylistically. Such liturgical focus is critical in the information age, which promotes inattention, empty rhetoric, and visual as well as aural manipulation. Too many churches, unaware of their own traditions, implicitly adopt the visual and aural chaos of society. As a result, worship does not so much help the faithful to relocate in reality as much as it further fragments congregants' lives. When worship is like flipping through the remote control or surfing the World Wide Web, it cannot direct believers to the spiritual self-discipline and biblical coherence they need.

Grasping Your Liturgical Tradition

1. When is silence important in worship?
2. How do you dialogue with God and among worshipers?
3. What are the *nonnegotiable* liturgical practices—and why?
4. How do you define the meaning of sacraments?
5. When, why, and how are music and singing used in worship?
6. What types of images and decorations are most fitting for your style of worship?
7. How does your worship space express your theological and biblical convictions?

Seeing and Hearing Well

Finally, fitting use of presentational technologies ought to improve the assembly's ability to see and hear without distraction or unintelligibility. This might seem obvious, but it is not. One step toward technological progress might weaken actual communication in worship space. The use of projected song lyrics, for instance, can make it more difficult for children to read the lyrics without standing on pews or chairs. Also, unless a congregation is given hymnbooks or provided with projected harmonies, the singing of classic hymns can atrophy (here again, some traditions, including Mennonites and the Brethren, have been particularly strong at this kind of singing). Also, young children are less likely to learn both the lyrics and music if they do not have printed music that parents can use to keep them on track. Seeing and hearing well in worship does not mean merely viewing a screen or hearing only the person who uses a microphone.

Conclusion

A gifted church music director told me about a worship service in which he integrated a wide range of styles, technologies, and practices—all within the context of his church's historical evangelical faith. The service began with the choir singing one of the psalms antiphonally from either side of the worship space. It then shifted to congregational singing of a popular worship song with the aid of projected lyrics. Next the congregation recited the historic Nicene Creed, again from the screen. The pastor's sermon about the mystery of the Trinity addressed the previous musical elements and the creed. The subsequent offering was an appropriate way of expressing that shared commitment publicly. A benediction from the Triune God was a reminder of who the congregation is, whose it is, and how it ought to live as it reenters the wider society.

Fitting worship, important today as always, has many dimensions, including practical, artistic, aesthetic, theological, liturgical, architectural, and seasonal. If we desire intimacy with God and neighbor in the dialogue of grace, we have to consider how presentational technologies can contribute to this intimacy.

6

Technological Stewardship

> Think of it as technological cocaine—so effortless to embrace initially, so difficult to relinquish after that. People who once use PowerPoint generally don't stop using it.[1]
>
> —Julia Keller

A southeastern seminary invited me to speak to a group of students who were examining the role of technology in the life of the church. The course meeting time conflicted with my schedule for teaching college freshmen, so instead of traveling there, I invited the seminarians to join my students in a live video dialogue.

When the two classes met via digital video, the seminarians wanted to know what my freshmen thought about the use of presentational technologies in worship. After some initial discussion, one of my undergraduates explained that her church was deeply divided on the issue because of what had happened when it purchased and installed a high-end presentational system. She recalled how her congregation was hopeful that the new technology would reinvigorate worship, especially for young members. By the time all was said and done, however, the cost of the new system was vastly over budget and the church was financially pressed. The church leaders finally decided that the only way to address the unexpected budget woes was to lay off one of the two full-time pastors. The congregation had spoken by default: technology was more important than a second pastor.

We were stunned. It was one of those rare moments in education where one illustration speaks volumes. We could not ignore the fact that technological decisions can have enormous implications for churches. When asked how her congregation eventually came to grips with what happened, my student said that most members just accepted the inevitable. I could not help but ask her what the new presentational system was being used for. Her response sent us all reeling once again: the church uses it only for musical lyrics and sometimes for sermon notes. Surely the congregation could have chosen a far less expensive means of projecting text on a screen.

I offer this story to highlight the stewardship implications of our technological pursuits in worship. Unless a church is willing to remain fairly low-tech, the cost of pursuing high-tech worship can become an ongoing burden as well as a blessing for churches—and not just financially. At issue is a host of financial, time, and opportunity costs that many churches never consider adequately before plunging into technological sophistication. A "one-size-fits-all" approach to worship technology is a major mistake. Here again, a moderate "yes, but" is usually better than a dogmatic "yes" or "no."

Technological Moderation

In the monastic tradition churches are also communities of surplus. Medieval monasteries nurtured community partly by creating a surplus of many things that people needed, from clothing and food to shelter, manuscripts, and especially love. All congregations can learn from this strategy by having the courage to say no to particular liturgical practices so that they are free to say yes to others. Especially important is moderation in technology-related costs, so that the congregation can sustain nontechnological activities as well.

Personal and community self-discipline in technological endeavors is necessary in order to maintain other aspects of ministry. Unless technological pursuits clearly challenge a congregation beyond its means, a church will tend to pursue unnecessary extravagance. This happens all the time.

Churches are willing to fund some expensive items over time, such as a piano, pipe organ, or church renovation. But too many congregations do not realize that digital technologies involve both short-term and long-term commitments.

Our survey discovered that the vast majority (over 90 percent) of all of the people who use media technologies in worship were "self-taught learn-as-we-go." Perhaps these are wonderfully gifted volunteers or paid staff who have taken up additional duties. Most likely congregations simply did not fund training. This is not good moderation; this is a lack of financial commitment to excellence in the use of technology in worship.

Typical Costs of Presentational Technologies

1. *Equipment* (screen, projector, video player, wiring, hardware, installation)
2. *Training* (artistic design, liturgical knowledge, technical expertise)
3. *Software* (file storage and organization, presentation)
4. *Legal* (copyrights for music, lyrics, and images)
5. *Maintenance* (hardware and software upgrades, repairs)
6. *Replacement* (new hardware and software every three years)
7. *Staff* (salaries, contract help, supervising volunteers)

The safest way to address technology-related costs is to practice reasonable moderation within the context of excellence—not perfection. Many consultants will advise that a church should spend as much as it can afford on presentational technologies to avoid disappointing performance and the need to replace equipment in the near future. In most worship spaces, however, higher-end equipment is unnecessary. A parish is better off spending a bit less on the technology and more on training people how to run it well and how to make appropriate choices within worship.

The Missionary Impulse

Church-growth movements frequently maintain strong commitments to spread the Good News. Indeed, many Christian forays into media technologies reflect a genuine, if at times excessive, emphasis on evangelism. Presentational technologies have become part of this missionary impulse to evangelize through worship services that are culturally relevant. "The technological revolution that is upon us is nothing more or less than a new mission field," writes one advocate of high-tech church-growth strategies, "and it is incumbent upon those of us who love the church and its Lord to 'ask the Lord of the harvest to send out laborers into his harvest' (Luke 10:2)."[2]

This missionary impulse raises two major dilemmas. First, evangelism itself is not an adequate basis for high-tech strategies in corporate worship. Worship is primarily for the community of believers to gather together thankfully to praise God, who alone is worthy of such adoration (Rev. 22:8–9). Certainly there is an evangelistic *aspect* to worship, and congregations ought to welcome warmly those visitors who are exploring whether or not they should worship God. But worship itself is not *primarily* for outsiders to the faith; it is meant for those already in a relationship with God and other believers.[3]

Therefore, approaching the use of presentational technologies in worship chiefly as an evangelistic enterprise is problematic. The practice can alter the God-glorifying nature of true worship. As stewards of worship, church leaders are obligated to ensure that the liturgy appropriately fosters thankful hearts, renewed minds, and weeklong praise in both work and play.

Some seeker-oriented churches use technology to appeal to visitors—but usually to gain new church members who then will be discipled within small groups and will participate in the "real" worship on another day. Even the Protestant reformer Martin Luther had a kind of seeker-driven notion that there should be different worship services for evangelism than for corporate worship.

The dilemma is that evangelistically oriented worship can interfere with a congregation's reverential praise of God. An emphasis on evangelistic worship can lead to liturgical techniques designed to entice and convert rather than worship—to make worship seem like something it is not. In some cases, worship begins to resemble propaganda or entertainment. Because it exists for a fundamentally different purpose—thankfully praising and drawing us closer to God—worship does need to be distinguished from what occurs in concert halls, theaters, and self-help gatherings.

Second, the use of presentational technologies in worship probably is not a stewardly approach to evangelism. Undoubtedly high-tech worship does appeal to some new believers and inactive church members, who might become active in a church that promotes relevant and inspiring worship. But relevant, inspiring worship can be found in low-tech and high-tech churches. While some congregations think that technology is *the* means of becoming relevant to younger generations, there is among some early adults a contrary return to orthodoxy and very low-tech, traditional liturgies.[4]

In other words, technology does not guarantee cultural relevancy or spiritual vibrancy in worship. There is no evidence that I know of that presentational technologies per se are effective in attracting nonbelievers and leading them to faithful involvement in a Christian community. There is some evidence that mass-mediated evangelism campaigns create a flurry of outreach activity among churches and parachurch groups, but in the end few people are actually discipled into active congregational participation.[5]

The Cost of Discipleship

An overemphasis on high-tech worship can create a mistaken impression about the actual costs of living faithfully. Faithfulness is not a matter of consumption—the easy use of manufactured images and sounds for individual gain. For all of their value to the individual, liturgical practices are also *costly* work, not "cheap grace."[6] The technological systems of modern society are oriented toward a secular concept of benefit expressed in the ideas of personal enjoyment, ease of understanding, and freedom of individual choice.

Worship needs to be evocative and inspiring, not impenetrable and stifling. But worship nonetheless requires personal and collective effort, even sacrifice. True worship of God entails relinquishing our own plans, agendas, and penchants. In worship we broken people go to God for healing, but the curing is not on our own terms. God does it God's way, not ours. Above all, worship repairs our relationship with the Creator by retuning our hearts to praise and thanksgiving rather than to selfish concerns. And the resulting wholeness leads us to lives of service. The whole intent of going to worship for "what I can get out of it" is contrary to what liturgy is intended to accomplish. The cost of authentic worship is also the gain: faith in a saving, self-sacrificial God rather than in our lost, selfish selves.

Whereas technology seems to promise us instant change and ready-made benefit, the biblical promises expressed in worship are related to whether or not worshipers live self-sacrificially. In the kingdom of God, the quality of worship depends on, among other things, believers' quality of life outside the sanctuary. Technology will not "work" as a technique to control God on Sunday mornings or any other time. In other words, the *kinds* of persons we are in worship shape what worship does *for* us or *to* us—or, more accurately, how *God* likely responds to us in dialogue.

The Old Testament prophets frequently hammered away at people who claimed to worship God but did not live justly. Some things never change in a fallen world. Too often our worship today is a kind of escape to God, accentuated by technologically enhanced feelings and emotions designed to make us feel good even as we live selfishly, without love of God and neighbor. We want to be close to God and to feel the Spirit's presence; we do not desire sacrifice, returning to God-the-giver everything that we have received. We too easily accept the cross of Jesus Christ without taking up our own crosses.

This might be why many churches today fail to include a confession of personal and collective sin in their liturgical practices—whether in prayer, music, reading, or otherwise. Worship tends to become more of a flight from the broken realities of the world and into personal happiness than an ongoing dialogue with God and neighbor for the sake of serving obediently.[7]

Authentic worship requires hard work and sacrifice. It demands that we give up our own penchants, programs, and quick fixes. It necessitates thinking not in terms of efficiency and control but in the language of faithfulness, obedience, trust, and especially love. We can evaluate worship partly on the basis of how well it equips people to invest their gifts and talents into God's kingdom for peace and justice beyond the sanctuary. Being stewards of worship includes attending to our community's responsibilities to the widow and orphan, to all of the victims of injustice. God saves for shalom, not for fun. We discover the abundant life as a covenant people "jointly pledged to travel together on the road to human flourishing—God blessing, the people exhibiting wisdom, righteousness, justice, love, and mercy."[8]

Stewards of Stillness

> Be still and know that I am God.
> I will be exalted among the nations.
> I will be exalted in the earth.
>
> Psalm 46:10

How can we foster stillness in worship? Do we set aside time for liturgical silence? Do we stand, sit, or kneel? How do we become intimate with God in the midst of the cacophony of messages that make up technological life?

The psalmist sees a relationship between tranquility and knowing God. Intimacy with God is not a matter of human busyness. It is a different kind of effort, an exaltation.

Our problem in a technological society is not merely that we are inundated and even overwhelmed by too many messages. Our lives become flurries of technique, races from one diversion to the next, nearly nonstop indulgences in mediated clatter and clutter. We awake to the clock radio, drive to work listening to music or news and reading the billboards, work in environments increasingly contoured by the omnipresence of e-mail and the World Wide Web, check messages on voicemail systems, carry cell phones here and there, and click through hundreds of television channels. Henri Nouwen recalls while motoring through Los Angeles that he "had the strange sensation of driving through a huge dictionary."[9] Are we living according to the noisy and fragmenting demands of technologies?

Long before the rise of digital technologies, Søren Kierkegaard addressed the fundamental issue at stake in a technological orientation to life. "Busyness, keeping up with others, hustling hither and yon, makes it almost impossible for an individual to form a heart, to become a responsible, alive self."[10] We turn into machinelike cogs in systems of sending and receiving messages. Our frenetic pace keeps us from recognizing and acting upon our calling as caretakers of God's shalom. "The word no longer communicates, no longer fosters communion, no longer creates community, and therefore no longer gives life," writes Nouwen.[11] Surely he overstates the case; grace yet abounds. Nevertheless, we do act as if this world belongs to us and is here merely for our own, hectic machinations.

It should not surprise us, then, that we are so vulnerable to the people and institutions that promise us more control, whether clever advertisers or misguided preachers. Our hectic pace gives us the sense that we are losing power; technology offers a seemingly sure way of regaining it. In worship, too, technology appears as the most efficacious way to regain our ability to command our futures.

In this society of escalating busyness and seductive appeals to personal control, stillness is anathema. What does it offer us of value? Power seems to come with speaking, sending, transmitting, presenting, shouting, and manipulating. Give us our remote controls! Our computer networks! Our search engines! Our PowerPoint! Worship, too, slips into a feverish mode, like television programming that never offers us three seconds of silence unless the power goes off or we hit the mute button. Silence strikes us as an error, a missed cue. We look immediately for an alternative diversion. Stillness seems useless.

As Kierkegaard suggests, however, stillness and its accompanying silence are critical for us to regain a view of reality in the midst of our motion. Stillness exposes us as fallen champions of our own destiny. We must preserve the stillness to maintain our God-given capacity to listen and thereby to be obedient. Ironically, the great communication technologies of our age rarely help us to be better listeners.

Both personal and corporate worship must reclaim stillness. God has already spoken; indeed, his primary agency is speech itself. We are called to be listeners before we are speakers. Good worship provides time for hearing the voice of God in the stillness of our dependence. "All genuine instruction ends in a kind of silence," writes Kierkegaard, "for when I live it, it is no longer necessary for my speaking to be audible." Unless we listen in stillness, we can lose track of God's voice.[12] The "doing" of corporate worship requires a rhythm between stillness and activity. If we approach presentational technology as another means of quickening the pace of worship or making liturgy even busier than it already is, we will have capitulated to the diversions of our age.

Avoiding Foolishness

We should beware of the technologizing of worship also because we are called to be stewards of wisdom. The opposite of wisdom is not a lack of information or technique, but *foolishness*. The great cost of foolishness is losing track of reality and sliding into self-delusion. The fool can be technologically skilled but has few clues about the overarching reality of life under the lordship of Jesus Christ. Such foolishness sets us off in one dead-end direction after another, including the search for quick fixes to the age-old problems of human nature, church growth, and spiritual discernment. Fools with tools are still fools.[13]

The greatest sign of foolishness in high-tech worship planning is a lack of humility about the long-term implications of importing technique into liturgy. Under the spell of new technologies, the fool places increased technical skill above all other goals. A worthy *telos* slips from her or his view. In worship, the fool embodies a truncated fascination with presentational tools as if they represent the alpha and omega of liturgical power. Admittedly foolishness is rarely the sole basis for launching the use of presentational technologies in worship. Still it lurks underneath all of a church's overly optimistic rhetoric about the power of technology to revolutionize worship for good.

Foolishness is evident in poor decisions about ministry. Fools spend more on technology than on missions programs. They ignore copyright issues, stealing online material with abandon. Fools budget for presentational technologies, including computers, but fail to consider the longer-term costs such as bugs that will need to be fixed, upgrades of software and hardware, and especially ongoing training in both technology and liturgy. They order projectors and screens before having discerned where to place them within the sanctuary or even whether or not the worship space is a fitting place for such tools. Fools implement new technologies with no clear and compelling argument for how the tools will actually improve worship or for what "improved worship" means. They hire technical consultants who know a great deal about machines but ridiculously little about worship.

Conclusion

The best way to avoid such a foolish lack of stewardship in our use of presentational technologies in worship is by cultivating wisdom. Yet such wisdom is hard to find. For one thing, the technologies are relatively new. We do not have enough experience to know with confidence how we should use them. For another, there is not much of a market for such wisdom; congregations like to talk about the benefits or even the necessity of presentational technology far more than they do about its wise use. After all, the wider society imagines that technology is *the* solution even if it cannot define the problem (*solutions* was one of the great buzzwords of the technology gold rush of the 1990s). To make our foolishness even worse, we are too apt to dismiss even moderate critics of worship technologies without listening to their potentially valid even if overstated concerns. Gaining wisdom is an inefficient process that requires a long obedience toward good, right, beautiful, and true worship action—fittingness in all senses.

Poor stewardship always is costly in the long run. It can dilute worship, burden current and future budgets, frustrate and dismay congregants, divide worship communities, cause grief to parish leaders, stymie worshipers' capacity to hear and obey, turn over liturgical decision making to imprudent consultants, and ultimately destroy a church's sense of its obligations to live out the gospel of peace. Whether or not such foolishness will be the tail that wags the dog in high-tech worship depends significantly on who is in charge. As Archbishop Charles J. Chaput wrote, "We certainly want salvation, and we acknowledge that salvation is of the Lord—but for many of us tools function as a pretty good insurance policy, just in case. . . . We've learned to trust our own ingenuity because it works. Unfortunately, the construction crew at Babel felt the same."[14]

7

Virtuous Authority

> To what degree have [worship planners] become "technologized"?[1]
>
> —Susan White

While talking with one of the audiovisual staff in a large congregation, my colleagues and I made a startling discovery. The church pastors did not decide their own sermon topics. Instead, the people who put together the worship presentations had the authority to make this crucially important judgment. The availability of particular visual material essentially dictated to the pastor the biblical texts and topics of worship. I realize that this sounds highly unlikely, and it must be a great exception to the rule even in the high-tech churches. But it is a symptom of a deeper problem, namely, confusion over authority for worship services that require a range of expertise.

The issue of liturgical authority is not related only to choices about whether or not to purchase and implement particular technologies. It also involves fundamental questions about *how* to implement new technologies, *when* to use them, and especially *who* should determine their use. Clearly these are issues of church authority.

This chapter highlights the dilemmas churches face in making decisions about using presentational technologies in worship. Someone or some group has to be in charge. The broader society is relegating increasing power to specialists, including technologists. In fact, one of the biggest complaints in large organizations is that a "computer person" or the "IT Department" dictates everyone else's technological practices. To some extent, we welcome these experts because we are stymied by the complexity of everyday technologies.

Should the church follow suit, trusting the technical experts? We need technical experts in many churches these days. At the same time, however, pastors are the shepherds, the spiritual leaders responsible for making sure that worship is God-glorifying and edifying. Technical experts who lack an understanding of worship need to submit their work to church leadership under the greater authority of Jesus Christ.

The New Technical Experts

Most of us over fifty years of age know that if we need our computer fixed we can go to our children or grandchildren. Often youth are the technological authorities, the experts who know how to "make it work." We should not be surprised, then, that in many churches young people are involved in running audio boards, digital presentations, video clips, tape duplicators, and VCRs. Youth seem to pick up more quickly on how to use new electronics, just as they do when it comes to learning another language.

Within most churches that use presentational technologies, a fairly small cadre of people is in charge of the equipment. These technical positions do not involve the kinds of projects that most congregants long to undertake. Generally speaking, parishioners do not mind giving this work to the technically inclined members of our churches.

At the same time, however, even multimedia ministry is likely to depend on a fairly wide range of talents. Michael Bausch calls it "a team sport that involves the contribution of many hands and minds" (see accompanying list).

The Multimedia Ministry Team

1. Dreamers who are "forward-looking"
2. Techies who "love to learn and talk about multimedia equipment"
3. Film buffs who "watch lots of movies in theaters and at home"
4. Music lovers and artists who include "photographers, artists, and art educators"[2]

Any list of those who collaborate on the use of presentational technologies in worship should include liturgical planners or at least those who know quite a bit about liturgy. But "worship literacy," if we should call it that, has fallen on hard times. Even a pastor or a worship-planning committee may not have a grasp on worship. Bausch writes, "Most worship teams have agreed that someone has final authority over what is seen and heard in worship, and this authority generally rests with the clergyperson responsible for the service. This is where the buck stops."[3] But final authority over decisions is not the same as having knowledgeable people involved in the planning. Moreover, final authority does not guarantee any wisdom about the process of high-tech worship.

From what I can tell, the technologizing of worship is directing planning in opposite directions. On the one hand, the need for specialized assistance is necessarily getting more of the laity or nonclergy staff involved in planning and executing some liturgical practices. In general this is a good development because it means that churches will rely upon a wider range of member gifts and will create a broader sense of ownership of liturgy "by the people." About two-thirds of the respondents to our survey of churches said that they decided to use media technologies in worship partly because of the availability of technical experts in the congregation.

On the other hand, the overall lack of understanding of worship within congregations is causing decision making about technology to be more diffuse, less liturgically informed, and more open to co-optation by even well-intentioned but nevertheless specialized interests. By ignorance and default, some churches are turning over too much authority for worship to people who know little about liturgical planning.

The best worship planning comes out of the congregation as it strives faithfully to meet the spiritual needs of friends and family and visitors. The same is true for the use of presentational technologies.

Tradition vs. Technique

An example of where tradition and technique can collide is the tension between *liturgists* (I use this term for those who *plan* the liturgy) and *technicians*. A fairly common understanding of liturgy—to which I hold—borrows liturgical practics and meanings from previous reformations and adapts them to new settings. Historical continuity is the underlying premise not because history is completely correct as a guide to all worship but rather because innovations have to be justified as better serving the purpose of worship in spirit and truth and for the edification of the entire congregation.

In other words, we ought not to alter how we conduct worship purely for the sake of change. Progress requires at least some wisdom from the past because we cannot find it entirely in the latest fads or in a future that has yet to arrive. Novelty and innovation always are considerations as a congregation strives for worship that is meaningful, but a concern for newness should not be the primary guideline for tomorrow's liturgical practices. Newer technologies do tend to be faddish, both as equipment and as technique.

The liturgical past encompasses not only yesterday or the last decade or even the last one hundred years. Liturgical history is part of the record of the church, the worship practices of the early church, and even the Hebrew holidays and religious rites that early Christianity borrowed and adapted as part of the continuity from ancient Israel to the early church.[4] One of the false assumptions about "traditional vs. contemporary" worship is that traditionalists should look just at the last century or so and advocates of contemporary worship should focus merely on the present. Tradition runs much deeper, and the liturgical riches to be found there are glorious.[5]

Biblical understandings of worship, developed throughout church history, are the best guides we have to the future of worship as long as we are willing to adapt them to new situations and cultural contexts. Anyone involved in preparing a service that will use presentational technologies needs to know far more than how to make the projector or the software work; she or he must not be indifferent to liturgical history and the age-old purpose of worship, or this person merely takes up the role of a technical expert, not a liturgical planner. Such experts might be technical volunteers, full-time staff, denominational leaders, or even pastors; their official role is inconsequential if all they do is adopt the cause of technique over tradition.

Focusing partly on tradition helps to steer us away from technological fads or individuals' high-tech penchants. Worship is not meant to reflect merely the personal stamps of some individuals—although it takes persons to plan liturgy. Personality oriented liturgy lacks the authority of tradition.[6] Worship planning will fail if it is wholly the domain of experts who are uninterested in the purpose and record of liturgy. "We live in a cult of experts who explain and solve," writes Eugene H. Peterson. Experts "deny or ignore the mysteries and diminish human existence to what can be managed, controlled, and fixed. . . . Pastors cast in the role of spiritual technologists are hard put to keep that role from absorbing everything else."[7] Pastors even can become "media moguls."[8]

In order to adapt technology to worship, we need not just technicians who understand equipment but also wise worship leaders and liturgical planning groups that understand what makes for intrinsically right and fitting rather than showy liturgy. Let me emphasize again that I am not suggesting that tradition is all that matters, since even tradition, too, is open to misinterpretation and can become a kind of idolatry especially if it is not held to the refining fire of Scripture. Instead, I am embracing the long-standing belief in much of Christianity that God works through both the biblical record of the early church and later church history to keep the flock faithful. God uses history even though it is not a comparable source of wisdom and certainly not a direct source of revelation. We can learn from those who have gone before us, just as so many fine preachers use Bible commentaries to help them discern the wisdom of the Scriptures, many denominations use creeds and confessions to catechize members, and seminarians study church history to understand everything from how the Scriptures were compiled to the particular beliefs within the various streams of Christianity.

Also problematic is the growing prevalence of visual symbols in worship that lack any continuity with those of the past. Screens cover crosses. In some cases, seasonal colors, vestments, and related liturgical adornments give way to projected "images of the week," and even these potentially wonderful new symbols might be discarded for good after they have served their short-lived purpose.[9] One director of multimedia ministries at a Lutheran congregation told me that her pastor normally does not even see the illustrations she has chosen for projection "until they pop up on Sunday." Digital media have created such an explosion in available material, especially images and information of all kinds, that access to texts is no longer linked to any kind of authority.[10] Information tends to overshadow knowledge and even wisdom—a problem I have called "informationism."[11]

Those who plan our liturgical actions need not be biblical scholars or degreed theologians, but they should know and love worship traditions, including those that shaped their own tribe. Ideally the laity would be just as important as the clergy in forming (and informing) public worship, but neither group should be free to act completely outside the guidance of tradition and the authority of the spiritual leaders of the parish.

John D. Witvliet's questions about the role of music in worship are just as valid for presentational technology: Do we have the imagination and persistence to develop presentations that nurture Christian worship? Do we have the imagination and persistence to make a presentation that truly serves the gathered congregation, rather than the marketing company that promotes it? Do we have the persistence and imagination to develop and then practice a rich understanding of artistic virtue?"[12]

I am not suggesting that worship should be stuffy, elitist, or static, only that it must take into account historical inheritances as well as congregational tastes. Traditions were at one time innovations, too; some of those precedents might contain the seeds of creativity that we need today. They are gifts that we should decline only when they prove insufficient for right and fitting worship. As my colleague Duane Kelderman likes to say, history, too, should get a vote at the table. Faithful people have gone before us. Why not listen to them as well as to ourselves?

Multimedia Ministers

The worship technology trade press says that many churches have reached a point where they need "media pastors" or "multimedia pastors." A technical systems designer who is also a musician says in *Worship Leader,* "Churches need a media pastor when the level of technology we want to use in our worship exceeds the capabilities of a volunteer crew." He defines this new position in terms of six responsibilities (see list). Some technology-intensive churches probably do need such a full-time employee, although a surprising number of churches carry on well with a team approach to worship planning. But what makes someone who holds this kind of position a *pastor* or *minister* with spiritual authority over worship-related decisions? If the person who plans the presentations is dealing with content and not just aesthetics, he or she should probably be a pastor or layperson who is biblically, theologically, and liturgically wise.

Responsibilities of a Multimedia "Minister"

1. Managing the sound, video, and computer projection team
2. Mentoring the crew technically and professionally and being a spiritual leader to them
3. Interfacing with the pastoral staff on all issues relating to technology support
4. Operating all of the equipment in the church
5. Being involved in the design of new technical systems
6. Making technology, parts, and repair purchases based upon a budget given for this purpose[13]

As I listen to discussions about multimedia pastors, I wonder how much of such a person's work is thought of as technique and how much is part of worship planning. Even the six-part description in the list above scarcely requires an ordained pastor—except possibly for being a spiritual leader to the technical crew (although even here we assume that the crew also is under the spiritual nurturing of the *congregational* pastor).

So here is my take on what makes for a virtuous multimedia pastor or minister:

Virtuous Traits for High-Tech Worship Planners

1. *Wisdom* acquired from biblical study, spiritual mentors, an understanding of church history, and a knowledge of liturgy
2. *Moderation* resulting from personal humility and ultimate trust in God rather than in machines and techniques
3. *Patience* anchored in a long-term view of God's covenantal promises, not in short-term, humanly devised quick fixes
4. *Love* of God and neighbor reflected in a joyful life, a heart for grace that abounds, and delight in fellowship
5. *Excellence* at planning, designing, and evaluating both the aesthetic and the theological aspects of presentation
6. *A collaborative spirit* reflected in humility, listening to others, encouraging volunteers/staff, and a sense of justice

Pastors should not abdicate their role in worship planning. Nor should they try to control the process. They must oversee it as needed to ensure vibrant, biblically sound, and heartfelt worship.

Conclusion

Churches ought not to let their technological yearnings—however well intentioned—undermine the authority of the church leadership. In the information age all areas of life are coming under the influence of autonomous specialists who deal in technique and information, not matters of the heart. In today's society we too quickly grant authority to technical experts who may not understand the bigger picture—in this case the purpose of worship.

The philosopher Martin Heidegger argued that technology is the new *metaphysic*—the modern religion.[14] Our faith in technical expertise can challenge the authority of God's Word and God's shepherds on earth. We look in every area of life—from sex to sports and religion—for the "right techniques" that will guarantee success, which is usually little more than personal self-fulfillment. We seek control, not humble obedience.

Instead of accepting such pragmatic individualism in our church structures and traditions, we need to regain a sense of the church as the organic body of believers living under the rule of Christ. Worship planning is not ultimately a technical skill—although parts of worship planning require technical expertise—but instead a kind of faithful use of personal gifts and talents in the greater cause of the kingdom of God.

8

Moving Forward Wisely

> [Our technological efforts should be] a pilgrimage of obedience, a mandated way to greater insight into the meaning of creation as the Kingdom of God.[1]
>
> —Egbert Schuurman

Using presentational technologies wisely in worship requires sound judgment about thorny issues that predate current equipment and contemporary worship styles. As I suggested earlier, in the Christian tradition gaining wisdom means getting a better grasp of reality, not merely knowing a skill. Sometimes only the prudent person or judicious community knows how to ask the right questions in search of such wisdom.

So in this final chapter I summarize the modicum of wisdom suggested in this book. I offer seven ways for us to move forward as faithful stewards of presentational technologies in worship.

1. Learn about Liturgy

I cannot stress this enough. Currently many believers, including some of those who serve on worship committees, know far more about technology than they do about good liturgical practices. Our technological skills are outpacing our liturgical wisdom. In order to adapt new technologies to fitting worship, we need to clarify what worship is as well as know how presentational technologies can be used well within worship. Otherwise we might find ourselves inventing new liturgical practices that are more didactic, entertaining, or attention-getting than God-glorifying.

As caretakers of worship we need to involve in planning a wide range of aesthetic, musical, technical, and leadership talents—all under the authority of the pastor and other spiritual leaders. Giving worship over to one or another expert—whether a technician or a theologian or even a specialist in liturgy—will not serve the congregation well. Much of the laity, too, should know enough about liturgy to participate meaningfully in worship planning as well as worship. Introducing presentational technologies in worship presents an opportunity for participants to learn about liturgy.

2. Borrow from Low-Tech as Well as High-Tech Worship

We can learn much about fitting liturgical practices from churches in other cultures. The Spirit is alive today especially in places like Central Africa and Latin America. Many churches are thriving with minimal technology. We can learn from them just as we can from the larger, high-tech congregations growing in North America. We might discover how to revive worship as dialogue, especially by looking at liturgy in oral cultures, where people love the spoken word, practice storytelling, celebrate antiphonal communication, and use musical expression that involves the entire body in the dance of life in Jesus Christ.

Most North American congregations now have members who are from such cultures. Why not invite them to become involved in our worship planning?

Vibrant worship nurtures congregational participation rather than passive consumption. It covets liturgy as an organic means for the community of faith to renew its covenantal obligations to God. In our age of multimedia blitzes on television, film, and stage, we need to remember that sometimes the most fitting worship follows a contrary dictum: "Less is more." Other times the fully orbed technological presentations can be just as meaningful, engaging, and dialogical. In either case, we likely will discover in low-tech assemblies part of the future of worship in North America.

3. Progress Slowly with New Technologies

The rapid pace of technological innovation in society is not necessarily an indication of social, cultural, or especially spiritual progress. Advertisements tell us that we are falling behind unless we have the latest gadgets in our lives. Why should we believe this kind of hyperbolic rhetoric when we know that our own message-intensive lives are so heavy-laden?

The full scope of benefits and drawbacks of high-tech worship are beyond our grasp. For instance, we do not know the long-term impact of these technologies on worship, although we do know that the arts have contributed enormously to worship for hundreds of years—both good and bad (images, like music, can express some of the best and worst theology and piety).

Nor do we know whether or not there is a faddish aspect to presentational technologies that will eventually pass, leaving only the more serious congregations committed to their use. My hunch is that all new technological developments have a short-term fling with popularity and eventually find some point of more fitting equilibrium. Perhaps we can find that fitting place without practicing poor stewardship.

Let's humbly approach a liturgical future that we cannot engineer ourselves. Using presentational technologies is a learning process, not an end in itself. We will make mistakes. In our misguided desire to impress others or to seize the technological moment, we might find ourselves slipping into foolishness. The more measured our response to new inventions, the more likely it is that we can gain some wisdom as we go.

Slower innovation gives congregations a chance to reflect on new practices and to adjust fittingly to less disruptive changes. Launching the use of presentational technologies at special services, for instance, might make a lot of sense for churches in which there is considerable concern about what might be lost in high-tech worship.

Three Crucial Low-Tech Practices for Congregations

1. *Hospitality*—welcoming others (Rom. 12:9–21)
2. *Friendship*—loving others self-sacrificially (John 15)
3. *Neighborliness*—serving nonmembers (Luke 15:11–32)

4. Consider the Quality of Fellowship

Used foolishly, presentational technologies can divert our attention away from community and toward individualism and consumerism. After all, the information age is also the era of special liturgies for particular types of worshipers.

Today many larger churches and some medium-size congregations are carving up their assemblies into subgroups based on demographics, musical or artistic taste, lifestyles (such as Saturday night worship), and the like. A survey by pollster George Barna found that 47 percent of those who attended worship were "self-focused," 29 percent were "god-focused," and 2 percent had no focus.[2] Even the laity today refers to "traditional versus contemporary" worship as clear and distinct alternatives—when, in fact, history shows that nearly all worship is a combination of continuity and innovation.

How can we use presentational technologies fittingly for both faithful worship and strong community life? The same ways that congregations have adapted to previous artistic and technological possibilities—from pipe organs to electric guitars, banners to stained glass. Usually the technologies most embedded in liturgy cause the greatest concern and lead to the most significant innovations.

Three crucial practices that should mark all Christian communities are hospitality, friendship, and neighborliness. Maybe we can use such practices as yardsticks for measuring the quality of community life in our churches. Then we can assess how well technology is contributing to or detracting from them.

5. Adapt the Old to the New and the New to the Old

As God's creation unfolds we have a growing number of options for conducting worship. We have to discern which practices hold enduring value and which ought to be discarded, which ones truly help a flock to praise with thanksgiving the one, true God.

Today some churches tend to oversimplify this task merely by blending the old and new. There is some wisdom in this approach, since it respects both innovation and tradition. But we ought not to blend anything—old or new—just because the result is relevance or impact.

The key to "blending" is to remember that good worship is *essential,* not *instrumental:* we worship because it is right, proper, and fitting to do so, not in order to achieve a practical goal or to produce particular results. The impact belongs to the Triune God, whose Holy Spirit even leads us to worship.

The narrowly instrumental view of worship, so prevalent in liturgical planning today, is absent in the Scriptures. This truncated notion of worship is largely a product of modern, industrial life—an attempt by fallen creatures to engineer human destinies and make even worship conform to human schemes.

The best liturgical work is above all grateful praise of God. It is fitting for the righteous (not the self-righteous) to praise God, says Psalm 33. We do not combine the old and the new merely to maximize effects on audiences but instead to be true to God and to one another. This is why we must adapt rather than merely adopt or reject new technologies.

6. Seek Sincere and Beautiful Worship

Our presentations can be fragrant offerings to God. We live in an age when many people think that beauty is found primarily in museums and galleries. They will drive hundreds of miles to view the artworks in a building donated by a patron and in settings controlled by elites. But they hardly expect such beauty in God's house. Surely we can do better.

Beautiful worship is meant for all believers, not for a privileged class of patrons, ticket-holders, intellectuals, theologians,

Beautiful and Sincere Worship

1. Are worshipers treated sincerely, without visual or aural manipulation?
2. Does the congregation participate in worship with a deep sense of sincere gratefulness to God and love of Jesus Christ?
3. Is the worship space, including all presentations and banners and other artwork—a joy to behold, inspiring and fitting for gathering before the face of our Lord?

or critics. Presentational technologies offer new ways of "capturing simple elegance" and "dignifying the ordinary."

Liturgical presentations ought to be sincere, not façades for the congregation or visitors. Our sincerity comes from knowing that our sins are forgiven (Lev. 26:13) and that we are serving God (1 Sam. 2:11). The Lord knows our hearts. Showy, artificial worship is an offense to the Lord. Well-done presentations are a sweet fragrance.

Conclusion

God calls us as worshipers to the work of liturgy, which is the single most important thing we can do as human beings. It establishes the living context for everything else we do. The heavens cry out to the glory of God. All of creation sings and displays such glory. So should we.

God invites us to worship; we accept the invitation. It is right and fitting to praise him. It is our joy and salvation that we should come together to hear the gospel, praise God's almighty name, confess our deep brokenness, proclaim our faith, hear God's Word, encourage each other in prayer, and leave in peace with God's blessing to love and serve the Lord.

In worship God transforms the ordinary into the extraordinary. There is no perfect liturgical presentation, but neither should there be mediocrity or a lack of reverential sincerity. Our many tasks in worship planning today include learning to adapt presentational technologies wisely for heavenly praise. Tradition can give us one guide. Scripture is critical. Creativity is essential. Virtue is vital. Hearts of sincere faith are golden.

Although we sometimes overestimate the value of new technologies in worship, we had better not underestimate their potential as well. Let the technically, artistically, and liturgically gifted all join together in planning and performing liturgy.

We can invest our whole being in worship—including our imaginations, curiosities, and abilities. This can be a glorious high-tech offering.

Appendix

A Snapshot of Technology in Churches

Important Motivations for Using Visual Media Technologies

Motivation	Percentage of Churches Surveyed
To gain contemporary relevance	84%
To gain youth relevance	77%
To evangelize	65%
To avoid print media	61%
To explore artful worship	59%
Could use members' gifts	59%
Had access to equipment	38%
To keep pace with others	33%

Important Methods for Training Members How to Use Presentational Technologies

Method	Percentage of Churches Surveyed
Self-teaching on the job	90%
Training by church staff	70%
Individual tutorials	50%
Professional training sessions	45%
Classes	29%

The data in this appendix are from a survey of all identifiable churches (an "n" of 330 from a total survey of 895 congregations) in the Michigan counties of Kent and Ottawa during the fall of 2002 and the spring of 2003. Figures have been rounded to the nearest whole number. *Visual media technologies* include all presentational technologies, from overhead projectors to computer-based projectors and film/35mm projectors. The full results of the study are online at the website of the Calvin Institute of Christian Worship (http://www.calvin.edu/worship/), which sponsored the research. The results also are reported in Steve Koster, *Visual Media Technology in Christian Worship* (masters thesis, Michigan State University, East Lansing, 2003).

Percentage of Churches Surveyed, Separated by Tradition, That Reject Visual Media Technologies

	Orthodox	Roman Catholic	Mainline	Evangelical
Computer	100%	94%	45%	34%
Video	100%	81%	43%	37%
Overheads	100%	100%	72%	54%
Film/35mm	100%	94%	78%	73%

Important Factors in Rejecting Use of Computer Projectors

Factor	Percentage of Churches Surveyed
Budget	59%
Lack of resources	46%
Tradition	42%
Lack of training	40%
No interest	37%
Majority opinion	30%
Minority opinion	28%
Time	25%

Media Types Used Weekly in Worship

Media Type	Percentage of Churches Surveyed
Text only	73%
Graphics and text	56%
Animation	14%
Live video	9%
Movie clips	4%
Congregational videos	3%

Liturgical Purpose of Using Visual Media Technologies in Worship

Purpose	Percentage of Churches Surveyed
Enhance attendees' participation	76%
Deliver information	59%
Create environment	55%
Teach concepts	37%
Use as a worship leader	5%

Notes

Introduction

1. Robert Phillips, "Proclamation and Worship in the 21st Century," *Southwestern Journal of Theology* 42 (summer 2000): 58.

Chapter 1: *Our Confusion*

1. Søren Kierkegaard, *Provocations: Spiritual Writings of Kierkegaard,* comp. and ed. Charles E. Moore (Farmington, Pa: Plough, 1999), 411.

2. Ivan Illich, *Tools for Conviviality*, ed. Ruth Nanda Anshen (New York: Harper & Row, 1973).

3. Louis Weil, *A Theology of Worship* (Cambridge, Mass.: Cowley, 2002), 111.

4. Eugene H. Peterson writes, "Spirituality digs wells deep into our traditions, and at some point, we find we have tapped into a common aquifer." He adds, "Recover what is yours by right by going deep, not away. The grass is not greener on the other side of the fence. Every religious community has its dead spots; your task is to dig wells in your desert." *Subversive Spirituality* (Grand Rapids: Eerdmans, 1997), 38–39.

5. These are nearly final data on a national survey of churches that colleagues and I conducted in 2003 with the support of the Calvin Institute of Christian Worship at Calvin College in Grand Rapids, Michigan.

6. Society of St. John the Evangelist, *The Rule of the Society of Saint John the Evangelist* (Cambridge, Mass.: Cowley, 1997), 36.

7. One of the most cogent expressions of this argument is Pierre Babin, *The New Era in Religious Communication* (Minneapolis: Fortress, 1991).

8. Doug Adams, quoted in Michael G. Bausch, *Silver Screen Sacred Story: Using Multimedia in Worship* (Bethesda, Md.: Alban Institute, 2002), ix.

9. Len Wlson, *The Wired Church: Making Media Ministry* (Nashville: Abingdon, 1999), 41.

10. Bausch, *Silver Screen Sacred Story,* 49.

11. See Patricia S. Klein, *Worship without Words: The Signs and Symbols of Our Faith* (Orleans, Mass.: Paraclete, 2000).

12. Rebecca Lyman, *Early Christian Traditions* (Cambridge, Mass.: Cowley, 1999), 67.

13. Ibid., 64.

14. Neil P. Hurley, S.J., "Telstar, Electronic Man, and Liturgy," *Worship* 39 (June/July 1965): 324.

15. See James W. Carey, *Communication as Culture: Essays on Media and Society* (Boston: Unwin Hyman, 1989), 13–36.

16. Bausch takes this definition from *The Dictionary of Multimedia*. See *Silver Screen Sacred Story*, 7.

17. For a brief but articulate explanation of worship as dialogue, see CRC Publications, *Authentic Worship in a Changing Culture* (Grand Rapids: CRC Publications, 1997), 39–40.

18. Craig M. Gay, *The Way of the (Modern) World: Or, Why It's Tempting to Live as If God Doesn't Exist* (Grand Rapids: Eerdmans, 1998), 293.

19. Richard Rohr, *Simplicity: The Art of Living* (New York: Crossroad, 1991), 56.

Chapter 2: *Understanding Worship*

1. Richard Winter, *Still Bored in a Culture of Entertainment: Rediscovering Passion and Wonder* (Downers Grove, Ill.: InterVarsity Press, 2002), 133.

2. Tim Eason, "The Software-Driven Church," *Church Magazine*, December 2000, http://www.churchmedia.net/CMU/articles/software/010.shtml.

3. Jacques Ellul, *The Technological Society* (New York: Vintage, 1964), xxv.

4. Barna's 2002 research is being reported in the following upcoming publication: *Music and the Church: Relevance in a Changing Culture* (Waco: Baylor University Press). A summary of the study is available online at http://www.barna.org.

5. Nicholas Wolterstorff, *Until Justice and Peace Embrace* (Grand Rapids: Eerdmans, 1983), 155.

6. Ernest Gordon, *To End All Wars* (Grand Rapids: Zondervan, 2002), 125.

7. H. Richard Niebuhr, *The Responsible Self* (Louisville: Westminster John Knox, 1999), 31.

8. A. W. Tozer, *The Pursuit of God* (Harrisburg, Pa.: Christian Publications, 1968), 73.

9. N. T. Wright, "Freedom and Framework, Spirit and Truth: Recovering Biblical Worship" (lecture, *January Series*, Calvin College, 11 January 2002). We have to see our technological capacity in "the light of this mandate to heal, to tend, and to produce an abundance for human beings (Luke 9:2; John 10:11)," says Cornelis Dippel. Cornelis Dippel, "Liturgy in the World of the Sciences, Technology and Commerce," in *Liturgy in Transition*, ed. Herman Schmidt, S.J. (New York: Herder and Herder, 1971), 104. The creation itself is "an act of imaginative love." Cornelius Plantinga Jr., *Engaging God's World: A Reformed Vision of Faith, Learning and Living* (Grand Rapids: Eerdmans, 2002), 23.

10. Samuel E. Balentine, *The Torah's Vision of Worship* (Minneapolis: Fortress, 1989), 91.

11. See Hugh Wybrew, *The Orthodox Liturgy: The Development of the Eucharistic Liturgy in the Byzantine Rite* (London: SPCK, 1989), 5–6.

12. Lyman, *Early Christian Traditions*, 101.

13. Don E. Saliers, *Worship Come to Senses* (Nashville: Abingdon, 1996), 14–15.

14. Nicholas Wolterstorff, "Justice as a Condition of Authentic Liturgy," *Theology Today* 48 (April 1991): 8.

15. David Peterson, *Engaging with God: A Biblical Theology of Worship* (Downers Grove, Ill.: InterVarsity Press, 2002), 250–53.

16. Lyman, *Early Christian Traditions*, 63–65.

17. For another perspective on the pre-denominational elements of worship as evident in church history, see Robert E. Webber, *The Worship Phenomenon* (Nashville: Abbott Martyn, 1994), 149–55; and Webber, *Worship Is a Verb* (Waco: Word, 1985), 47–66.

18. Of course the nonnegotiables of the Christian faith are always "contextualized in" or "mediated through" a particular culture and even via a local congregation. Nevertheless, there is a historical reality to the gospel and therefore to worship that is anchored in the gospel. God reveals the truth of the gospel through the Scriptures and through the Word made flesh, Jesus Christ.

19. James B. Torrance, *Worship, Community & the Triune God of Grace* (Downers Grove, Ill.: InterVarsity Press, 1996), 56.

20. William H. Willimon, *The Service of God: Christian Work and Worship* (Nashville: Abingdon, 1983), 56.

21. Craig Dykstra, *Growing in the Faith: Education and Christian Practices* (Louisville: Geneva, 1999), 91.

22. For a review of the literature on liturgy and aesthetics, see John D. Witvliet, "Toward a Liturgical Aesthetic: An Interdisciplinary Review of Aesthetic Theory," *Liturgy Digest* 3, no. 1 (1996): 4–87.

23. Richard R. Gaillardetz, *Transforming Our Days: Spirituality, Community, and the Liturgy in a Technological Culture* (New York: Crossroad, 2000), 94.

24. Jaroslav Pelikan, *The Vindication of Tradition* (New Haven: Yale University Press, 1984), 65.

25. G. Stephen Blackmore, "New Worship Media for New Generations," *Christian Ministry* 28 (April 1997): 20. Our English word *tradition* comes from the Latin verb *tradere,* which means "to hand on." See Lyman, *Early Christian Traditions,* 3.

Chapter 3: *Corporate Worship and Technology*

1. Robert Phillips, "Changes in Technology," *Southwestern Journal of Theology* 3 (summer 2000): 57.

2. Susan J. White, *Christian Worship and Technological Change* (Nashville: Abingdon, 1994), 36.

3. Ibid., 64ff.

4. Carl Mitcham, *Thinking through Technology: The Path between Engineering and Philosophy* (Chicago: University of Chicago Press, 1994), 129.

5. Nathan D. Mitchell, "The Amen Corner," *Worship* 75 (September 2001): 472.

6. Neal Gabler, *Life the Movie: How Entertainment Conquered Reality* (New York: Random House, 1998), 1.

7. Winston Churchill, quoted in "Parliamentary Debates," Fifth Series, Volume 393, *House of Commons Official Report,* Ninth Volume of Session 1942–43, 28 October 1943 (London: His Majesty's Stationary Office, 1943), 403.

8. Quoted in Eileen Crowley-Horak, "Testing the Fruits: Aesthetics as Applied to Liturgical Media Art" (doctoral diss., Union Theological Seminary, New York, 2002), 75.

9. Phillips, "Changes in Technology," 56.

10. Bob Pittman, quoted in Quentin J. Schultze et. al., *Dancing in the Dark: Youth, Popular Culture, and the Electronic Media* (Grand Rapids: Eerdmans, 1991), 192.

11. Wright, "Freedom and Framework, Spirit and Truth."

12. For a summary of the argument that human beings are called to be responsible servants to God, see especially Nicholas Wolterstorff, *Art in Action: Toward a Christian*

Aesthetic (Grand Rapids: Eerdmans, 1980), 74–76. The role of "media art" in worship is discussed in Crowley-Horak, "Testing the Fruits," 9ff.

13. Wolterstorff, *Until Justice*.

14. For an analysis of Augustine's place in the history of rhetoric, see George A. Kennedy, *Classical Rhetoric and Its Christian and Secular Tradition: From Ancient to Modern Times* (Chapel Hill: University of North Carolina Press, 1980), 149–60. Also see Garry Wills, *Saint Augustine* (New York: Penguin, 1999), 45.

Chapter 4: *Avoiding Quick-Fix Techniques*

1. Robert E. Webber, *Worship Old and New: A Biblical, Historical, and Practical Introduction,* rev. ed. (Grand Rapids: Zondervan, 1994), 106.

2. I develop this argument more fully in *Habits of the High-Tech Heart: Living Virtuously in the Information Age* (Grand Rapids: Baker Academic, 2002).

3. Eugene H. Peterson, *The Contemplative Pastor* (Carol Stream, Ill.: CTI, 1989), 72.

4. Marva Dawn, *Powers, Weakness and the Tabernacling of God* (Grand Rapids: Eerdmans, 2001).

5. Kathleen A. Cahalan, "Technology and Temperance," *Chicago Studies* 41 (spring 2002): 30.

6. Marva J. Dawn, *A Royal "Waste" of Time: The Splendor of Worshiping God and Being Church for the World* (Grand Rapids: Eerdmans, 1999), 123.

7. One such development is the "simplicity movement."

8. Quoted in Sally Morgenthaler, "Worship and Technology: Beyond the Hype," *Worship Leader*, Technology Issue (2001).

9. For a helpful perspective on the impact of didacticism on liturgy, see Wolterstorff, *Until Justice,* 158.

10. White, *Christian Worship,* 101. Kathleen Norris suggests that when "worship facilitators" gain control over worship, it "becomes sluggish, like a bad poem, with the weight of ideas, the gravity of political ideology." Norris recalls Emily Dickinson's despair over "relentlessly educational" worship that views paradise as nothing more than an "endless Bible school." "Like language," concludes Norris, "worship resists and transcends overt attempts at manipulation." Kathleen Norris, *Amazing Grace: A Vocabulary of Faith* (New York: Riverhead, 1998), 247–48, 250.

11. Quoted in J. D. Biersdorfer, "Religion Finds Technology," *New York Times* (16 May 2002), http://www.newyorktimes.com/2002/05/16?technology/circuits/16CHUR.html (22 May 2002).

12. Josef Pieper, *Leisure: The Basis of Culture* (South Bend, Ind.: St. Augustine's, 1998), 58, 68.

13. Harold M. Best, *Music through the Eyes of Faith* (San Francisco: HarperCollins, 1993), 57.

14. Dawn, *A Royal "Waste" of Time,* 233.

15. Ian Barbour, *Science and Secularity: The Ethics of Technology* (New York: Harper & Row, 1970), 68–69. "Technology is reliable, efficient, trustworthy, and offers us such control that a Faustian bargain seems the only logical precondition." Ronald Cole-Turner, "Science, Technology, and Mission," in *The Local Church in a Global Era: Reflections for a New Century*, ed. Max L. Stackhouse, Tim Dearborn, and Scott Paeth (Grand Rapids: Eerdmans, 2000), 102.

16. Peterson, *Subversive Spirituality,* 211.

17. Dawn, *A Royal "Waste" of Time,* 102.

Chapter 5: *Fitting Technology into Worship*

1. Mitchell, "The Amen Corner," 254.

2. I have borrowed this concept of "fittingness" from Wolterstorff, *Art in Action,* especially pages 184–91.

3. Dorothy C. Bass, *Receiving the Day: Christian Practices for Opening the Gift of Time* (San Francisco: Jossey-Bass, 2000), 109.

4. Bausch, *Silver Screen Sacred Story,* 107.

5. Wolterstorff, *Art in Action,* 187.

6. She suggests five functions of liturgical media art: (1) to create an environment for worship; (2) to convey information; (3) to reinforce communication (4) to encourage participation; and (5) to invite relationship with God-in-the-world. Crowley-Horak, "Testing the Fruits," 85.

7. Emily R. Brink, "Gizmos and Grace: One Example of How New Technology Can Help Worship Leaders," *Reformed Worship* 44 (June 1997): 2.

8. Lyman, *Early Christian Traditions,* 5.

9. Robb Redman, *The Great Worship Awakening: Singing a New Song in the Postmodern Church* (San Francisco: Jossey-Bass, 2002).

10. John D. Witvliet, *Worship Seeking Understanding: Windows into Christian Practice* (Grand Rapids: Baker, 2003), 203–29.

Chapter 6: *Technological Stewardship*

1. Julia Keller, "Killing Me Microsoftly," *Chicago Tribune Magazine,* 5 January 2003, 11.

2. John P. Jewell, *New Tools for a New Century: First Steps in Equipping Your Church for the Digital Revolution* (Nashville: Abingdon, 2002), 12.

3. The early church had an all-encompassing approach to evangelism that took advantage of networks of friends, relatives, and neighbors. See Robert E. Webber, *Journey to Jesus: The Worship, Evangelism, and Nurture Mission of the Church* (Nashville: Abingdon, 2001), 29–42; Webber, *Celebrating Our Faith: Evangelism through Worship* (San Francisco: Harper & Row, 1986); Michael Green, *Evangelism in the Early Church* (Grand Rapids: Eerdmans, 1970).

4. See Colleen Carroll, *The New Faithful: Why Young Adults Are Embracing Christian Orthodoxy* (Chicago: Loyola Press, 2002).

5. See chapter 7 in Quentin J. Schultze, *Televangelism and American Culture: The Business of Popular Religion* (Grand Rapids: Baker, 1991).

6. Dietrich Bonhoeffer, *The Cost of Discipleship* (New York: Macmillan, 1963), 46–47.

7. Wolterstorff, *Until Justice,* 9–10.

8. Ibid., 17.

9. Henri J. M. Nouwen, *The Way of the Heart* (New York: Ballantine, 1981), 31.

10. Kierkegaard, *Provocations,* 19.

11. Nouwen, *The Way of the Heart,* 5.

12. Kierkegaard writes, "It is absolutely unethical when one is so busy communicating that he forgets to be what he teaches." *Provocations,* 85.

13. Charles J. Chaput, "Fools with Tools Are Still Fools," *Nuntium* (June 1998), http://www.archden.org/archbishop/docs/foolswithtools.htm (26 October 2001).

14. Charles J. Chaput, "*Deus ex Machina:* How to Think about Technology," *Crisis* 16 (October 1998): 19.

Chapter 7: *Virtuous Authority*

1. White, *Christian Worship,* 36.

2. Bausch, *Silver Screen Sacred Story,* 76–80.

3. Ibid., 85.

4. A helpful summary of the history of worship is in Robert E. Webber, *Worship Old and New*, 208–11.

5. For an analysis of the weaknesses of the "contemporary vs. traditional vs. blended" worship taxonomy, see Lester Ruth, "A Rose by Any Other Name: Attempts at Classifying North American Protestant Worship," in *The Conviction of Things Not Seen: Worship and Ministry in the 21st Century*, ed. Todd E. Johnson (Grand Rapids: Brazos, 2002), 34–36.

6. White, *Christian Worship,* 54.

7. Peterson, *Contemplative Pastor,* 72.

8. William H. Willimon, *Pastor: The Theology and Practice of Ordained Ministry* (Nashville: Abingdon, 2002), 56–58.

9. According to one study, the most frequent use of the Internet by "spiritual leaders" is finding resources for worship. See Elena Larsen et. al., "Wired Churches, Wired Temples: Taking Congregations and Missions into Cyberspace," Pew Internet & American Life Project (December 2000): 19, http://www.pewinternet.org/.

10. Tim Stratford, *Liturgy and Technology* (Cambridge, England: Grove Books, 1999), 13.

11. Schultze, *Habits of the High-Tech Heart,* 26–30.

12. John D. Witvliet, "Beyond Style: Rethinking the Role of Music in Worship," in Johnson, *The Conviction*, 73–77.

13. Donald C. Cicchetti, "Is It Time for a Media Pastor? Combining Technology and Ministry," *Worship Leader* (summer 2000): 23–24.

14. See his essay on "The Question Concerning Technology," Martin Heidegger, *The Question Concerning Technology and Other Essays,* trans. William Lovitt (New York: Harper Torchbook, 1977), 4–35.

Chapter 8: *Moving Forward Wisely*

1. Egbert Schuurman, "A Christian Philosophical Perspective on Technology," in *Theology and Technology: Essays in Christian Analysis and Exegesis,* ed. Carl Mitcham and Jim Grote (Lanham, Md.: University Press of America, 1984), 118.

2. Terry Jo Ryan, "Report Sheds Light on Beliefs," *Waco Tribune-Herald Tribune* (8 October 2002): 3B.